WALKING WITH FATHER VINCENT

To my family

Walking with Father Vincent

Andrew McNabb

GRACEWING

First published in England in 2023
by
Gracewing
2 Southern Avenue
Leominster
Herefordshire HR6 0QF
United Kingdom

www.gracewing.co.uk

ISBN 978 085244 711 6

Graphic "Boots" by Pat McNabb

Typeset by Word and Page, Chester, UK
Cover design by Bernardita Peña Hurtado

INTRODUCTION

Once a week, from some time in the 1920s to some time in the 1940s, a wiry old man would walk through the London streets wearing a coarse white and black Dominican habit that he had hand-woven himself. He also wore heavy black boots. He was on his way from his priory at the far northern end of the city all the way to Hyde Park, where he would preach near the Marble Arch at Speakers' Corner. There he was always greeted ... by hecklers. He patiently and joyfully dealt with all of them, calling the people in Hyde Park the best audience in the world. He silenced one heckler by stopping the speech, stepping down from the rostrum, and kissing the heckler's feet. Another man heckled him persistently—for twenty-five years! He gathered so many stories about his give-and-take with the old priest that he wrote an entire book about it. And though he conceded nothing in his arguments, his great respect for his opponent was evidenced by the title of the book: *A Saint in Hyde Park.*

While Fr. Vincent McNabb's public preaching invited hecklers, his holiness was a sufficient answer to silence his critics. People came from all over the world to attend his spiritual retreats and to hear his regular lectures at St Dominic's Priory. It was worth it, they said, just to hear him read from the scriptures before his talked. But then he illuminated the biblical texts with profound insight, always explained with humor and simplicity. For example:

> The "Our Father" ... at once gets our desires in order. It gives us our end. What is more fundamental in our life

> than getting our desires in order? Very few desires in our life are wrong in themselves. It is only that they are out of place.
>
> Prayer is almost the easiest thing in the world. Our blessed Lord tells the Apostles they should pray always, therefore it must be easy. If our blessed Lord says we must pray always, it is no business of anybody's to set that aside.

There was an incomparable quartet of Catholic writers who appeared in England in the early twentieth century: G. K. Chesterton, Hilaire Belloc, Ronald Knox, and Vincent McNabb. It is a marvel to contemplate that these spiritual, intellectual, and literary giants all lived in the same time and place and knew each other. Two of them were converts, two of them were journalists, two of them were priests, two of them wrote detective stories, three of them shared a passion for the implementation of Catholic Social Teaching, all four of them were master defenders of the Catholic faith, and all were prophetic in calling out the coming attacks on the family. They continue to be as timely and transcendent as ever.

Msgr. Ronald Knox said that Fr. McNabb was the only person he had ever met who gave him the feeling of what a saint must be like.

G. K. Chesterton hailed Fr. McNabb as "almost the greatest man of our time." He said, "I would hardly have become a Catholic if I had not recognized in him one of the few great historic heroes of Christianity."

For his golden jubilee, Fr. McNabb had planned to walk all the way to Rome. He had written to Belloc for advice and Belloc's letter in response was later found in Fr. McNabb's copy of *The Path to Rome.* His Dominican superiors, however, forbade him to make the walk. He was too valuable to them in London.

A champion of the Catholic Land Movement, Fr. McNabb urged people to live the life of Distributism (or what we now call localism). He was an ardent critic of industrialization, urban waste, public education, and all the modern innovations which did nothing but complicate people's lives, making them less religious, less independent, less happy. "I love liberty, to give it rather than to have it. I would be content to be a slave that others could be free." The articles he wrote for Chesterton's papers, the *New Witness* and *G. K.'s Weekly*, were always submitted on scraps of paper and mailed in recycled, inside-out envelopes.

In June of 1936, when Fr. McNabb heard that Chesterton was seriously ill, he rushed to the town of Beaconsfield to visit his friend. He knew immediately that Chesterton was dying. He sang the *Salve Regina* over him, and—in a scene for the ages—picked up Chesterton's pen from the bedside table and kissed it. He honored that pen and the man who had wielded it like a sword. Knowing Chesterton, he said, was like knowing St. Thomas Aquinas personally. "There is hardly a line of his writings that does not say to me with emphasis: 'This man is a philosopher.' But there are few if any lines that do not say with equal emphasis: 'This philosopher is a poet.'"

I've had the privilege of being involved in the revival of interest in Chesterton, and Belloc's resurgence has followed in that wake. Many good things have happened because of people reading and re-reading these two profound writers. Knox also needs to be rediscovered: his retreats, and his sermons, and his exquisite translation of the Bible. But the world especially needs to be invited to listen again to the little priest from the Order of Preachers, the holy man who demonstrated the truth of his serene and certain words with the witness of his daily life. Here is a book that takes an important early step in the McNabb revival. And fittingly, it is written by a McNabb. The personal connection is priceless. And what better way to get to know Fr. McNabb than by taking a walk with him? He will lead us to treasure, this priest who lived out his vow of poverty and humility in every step he took, the poor man who flung jewels to the whole world.

Dale Ahlquist
President, The Society of Gilbert Keith Chesterton

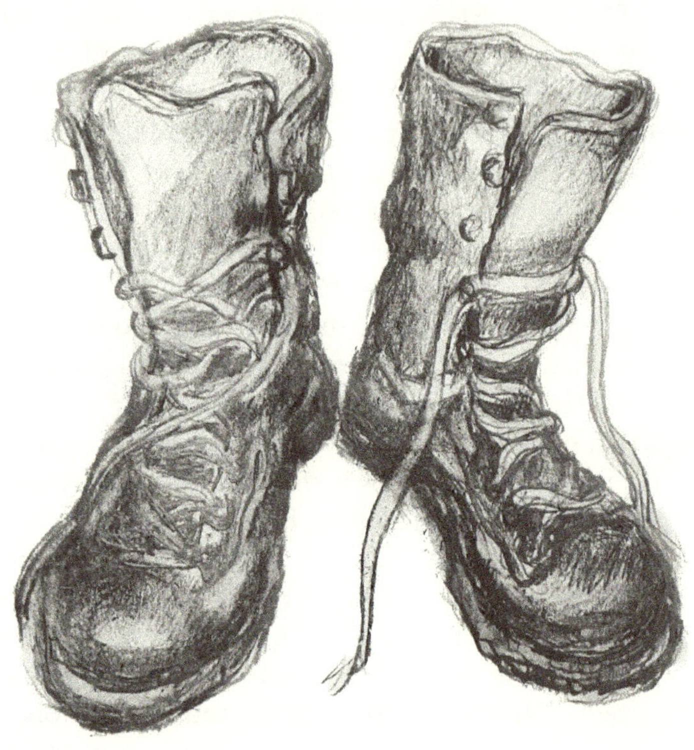

Buy boots you can walk in. Walk in them. Even if you lessen the income of the General Omnibus Company, or your family doctor; you will discover the human foot. On discovering it, your joy will be as great as if you had invented it. But this joy is the greatest, because no human invention even of Mr. Ford or Mr. Marconi is within a mile of a foot.

Father Vincent McNabb

Walking with Father Vincent

FOR DECADES, Father Vincent McNabb had the most recognizable feet in London. He was a fixture on the streets, walking everywhere he went, moving quickly through the crowds in his worn Dominican habit and heavy, black boots. "Some knew he was a Friar Preacher," a fellow Dominican wrote, "others, unaware that the thirteenth century was alive in their midst, thought he was a circus man."[1]

The lean, ascetic face, the hand-woven woolen habit, the limp black hat turned green from age and slung over his shoulder, his self-described "McNabb-sack," containing just the Bible and notes for preaching. But it was those old boots, handmade of English leather and "a sermon to all on his social doctrine of the crafts,"[2] that, upon full inspection of the man, struck so many.

"Father Vincent belonged to London," wrote Maisie Ward, co-publisher of Sheed & Ward, and a leading writer and intellectual of the day. "His convent lay in a deeply poverty-stricken area and ... moving among these folk of his, covering the several miles that lie between them and Hyde Park, he used to always go on foot, in big black boots, usually broken at the sides—for thus he kept literally his vow of poverty."[3] But really, those boots were evidence of a more varied commitment; to frugality, yes; to craftsmanship, indeed; but to a vigorous pursuit of souls, most of all.

"He took great pride in his old boots," wrote Edward A. Siderman in *A Saint in Hyde Park*, his literary tribute to his decades-long adversary at Speakers' Corner, "which he would wear until they all but dropped off his feet." And Father Vincent knew, himself, his boots were a talking point. One time, responding to a question from his audience about his boots, he said, "These boots are not very smart but they are handmade by a craftsman and are very comfortable and will last for years. I must have good boots." And, stating what they all already knew, "I walk a lot."[4]

A glimpse of his boots can be seen in the full-length portrait of a standing Father Vincent, painted by the famed portraitist Sir James Gunn. Gunn proclaimed him a wonderful sitter, remarking, though, that he refused to sit down at all, "but remained standing for periods of an hour-and-a-half after having walked [five miles] from Highgate to the studio in Pembroke Walk." This, of course, meant a five-mile walk back.

While his best-known path was the miles he trod most Sundays from the Dominican priory at Haverstock Hill to Speakers' Corner at Hyde Park to give his testimony at the Catholic Evidence Guild, it was known that he walked—and only walked if he could help it; and he usually could—to get where he was going. His walking was so well known that one time, fearing he would miss the requiem Mass for Fr. Bede Jarrett, O.P., his beloved prior, he hopped on a bus with a number of his brethren at their urging and to his great consternation, and a reporter caught whiff of it. "The same evening, *The Oxford Mail* published the story of how Father Vincent had broken his Golden Rule."[5]

His feet brought him to the city's convents to give retreats, into the back rooms of pubs to speak to the doubtful, to street corners in London's East End to preach impromptu and into Communist Cellars and debate halls, and more often than many people knew, into the homes of widows and the poor. He walked throughout the countryside at Ditchling, where he inspired craftsman, led Dominican tertiaries and encouraged those aspiring to live a life rooted in "First Things." He sought permission to walk to Rome from London, and often dreamed of walking to the Holy Land. He walked in all weather, and all times of day or night, right up to his very last days.

His walking, though, was hardly the only notable aspect of an extraordinary life. He was revered by Gilbert Keith Chesterton, who remarked, "Father Vincent McNabb is spiritually the greatest man in England at this time,"[6] and Hilaire Belloc, who said, "Never have I seen holiness in such scale,"[7] and Msgr. Ronald Knox, who said, "There was a kind of light about his presence which didn't seem to be quite of this world."[8]

Father Vincent was an adversary and debater of the poet, playwright and activist George Bernard Shaw. Prominent poets of the time, Maurice Baring and William Richard Titterton wrote poems about him. Sir James Gunn was not the only one to paint his portrait; Clarence White did, too, and that portrait was exhibited by the Royal Academy.

Babies were named for him at their baptism (several went on to become priests themselves), the poor adored him, Communists and Socialists steered clear of him. He was a fearless and unrelenting social critic, advocating for the economic theory Distributism and the Catholic Land movement. He railed against corporate greed and stood up for workers' rights. He worked hard for Christian unity and ecumenical relations, and was a leading voice against birth control and abortion decades before these would be hot-button topics. The King of Belgium bestowed on him the high honor of Chevalier of the Order of the Crown of Belgium, Pope Pius X prayed over him, and the Anglican Archbishop of Canterbury prayed on his knees beside him. He earned the highest degree possible in the Order, Master of Sacred Theology. He was an ascetic and a prophet, a theologian and a writer, a teacher and a Thomist and, to many, quite possibly a saint. And while not without controversy and even, at times, contradiction, he was frequently misunderstood, and misinterpreted, and even derided as a showman and an eccentric. But above all, he was a tremendous lover—of the Lord and his fellow man, and his life is testimony to that; this priest who, more than anything, as his biographer wrote, "Wanted to bring an erring world to its senses before it was too late."[9]

It is that statement that best summarizes Father Vincent's life. He approached every day with that impetus, rooted in his great awareness and understanding that humanity was heading down a very dark path. Much of what Father Vincent warned of—a world impersonalized, the family marginalized, our faith relativized and depleted—has sadly come true. What would he have to say today?

A lot.

And all of it can be viewed in light of his focus on the sanctity of the family, and in the context of his Dominican vocation. In his journeying, and in his activity, he was like his spiritual master, St. Dominic, a great walker himself, who crisscrossed Europe on foot, converting souls. A fellow friar summarized Father Vincent's Domincanism this way:

> Only those who can accept [Father Vincent] as a piece, whole and complete, will be able to see the reincarnation of St. Dominic, the contemplative preacher. The external manifestation of the Dominican life, the fearless wearing of his habit, the bare poverty of his cell, the booted trudging of the London streets . . . Father Vincent has shown that St. Dominic is up to date. The true contemplative is always contemporary.[10]

Yes, Father Vincent McNabb was a true contemplative and is thus, as his brother friar said, *always* contemporary. And so it is that one can *still* walk with Father Vincent. In fact, I have been trying. He was my great-granduncle, and I have been attempting to walk with him my entire adult life.

TO SAY FATHER VINCENT holds a place of prominence in my family would be accurate, but incomplete. I grew up hearing about the brother of my great-grandfather, Patrick McNabb (who emigrated to Boston), of course, and was glad to know I had a somewhat famous relative. There were the broad-brush strokes of the smart, eccentric Dominican who spoke weekly at Hyde Park, the stories of him sleeping on the floor of his cell, walking everywhere he went, being involved in a back-to-the-land movement, and his being a close friend of someone named Chesterton. But the depth of his greatness, I would later come to understand, really resided in something deeper, and that was never quite imparted.

So, where did that *something deeper* come from? God, ultimately. But family is not to be discounted. This is not a family book, per se, though family is a running thread. This is only fitting as the Holy Family was at the essence of Father Vincent's thinking, his preaching and, essentially, his life. It was a "Return to Nazareth" that so motivated him, was so essential to his understanding of that Christian truth: the family is the basic unit of society, is sacred, and as families go, so society goes.

Much of the good fruits that descended on Father Vincent and have cascaded the generations since are rooted in the piety and strength of his mother, my great-great grandmother, Ann (Shields) McNabb, of Rathmullan, Donegal. If there is one aspect of her life that encapsulates the woman, it is this: she emigrated to New York as a young woman, found immediate success, but uncomfortable with the trappings of wealth and fearing the loss of her soul, returned to Ireland.

Simply stated, this is stunning.

Ann Shields attained, in short order, the American Dream and rejected it. When thousands of Irish were leaving the country for *exactly* what she had found, she did the unthinkable. In Father Vincent's book, *Eleven, Thank God*, a tribute to his mother (the title coming from her proud response when asked how many children she had) he wrote of his mother's experience:

> Whatever the cause, Ann Shields, still in her teens, was allowed by her father to go with so many of her countrywomen to New York. But unlike so many, she was specially safeguarded. Her brother was first-mate on the ship. Her married sister had a home for her in New York.
>
> She was not long in making what might be called a successful beginning in life. With her wonted directness she asked to see the proprietor of one of the large millinery and dressmaking establishments in New York. The proprietor, seeing the slight Irish lass still in her teens, smiled as he suggested that in his business there was no place for an untried lass like her. But she said quite confidently, "If you let me do something for you, you will give me a place."
>
> It was not boasting, for I never knew her to boast. It was the expert's knowledge that one knows—which may or may not be humility, but is truth. In this case truth prevailed. The proprietor asked her to make something. When he saw what she had made he gave her a place. Before a twelvemonth was out he had given her a place at the head of her department.
>
> As she still had unflagging powers of work and unusual skill her master soon found her value to his establishment. Because he himself could not go to the yearly visit to Paris, made by the first-line establishments, he soon found that his young head of department was almost better than a Parisian expert. No sooner were the new Parisian models to be seen in these first-line establishments than his young head of department paid them a visit and, in a day, had reproduced—without the expense of a journey to Europe—all their Parisian models.

> ... then began what I surmise to be the untold drama of her life. Few of the thousands who had come West for a living, if not for wealth, had her chances of entering by business, or marriage, into America's wealthy classes.

Father Vincent goes on to write of her numerous marriage proposals, including from the son of the proprietor of that shop. But one day, while kneeling in prayer,

> Light came to her as she knelt. It was clear to her that to fight God's enemy in the city that offered her wealth at the cost of faith was to fight Satan on his battlefield, where the battlefield would give him the victory. Thus, she was driven by the Spirit [back] into the desert [Ireland], where on God's battlefield victory might not be hers; but would be possible.
>
> When she told her master that she had made up her mind to go home, his sense of her value asserted itself with fresh offers. When he had finally offered to make her a partner in the business, and she had refused he realized that some motive more than wealth-making was in the soul of this delicate girl in her teens.
>
> When God and her conscience bid her return to the safety and comparative poverty of her home none of the worldly advantages that were proving so fatal to the souls of her countrywomen in America could stay her return.
>
> She sometimes told us, in almost dull narration, that when she went to her cabin in the ship she found it was filled with flowers from her old master and from one or more of those who had hoped to one day call her wife. Flowers she always loved. But it never entered her guileless heart that these flowers were a wreathe of victory."[11]

When mentioning his mother's "almost dull narration," Father Vincent is highlighting her humility, of course, but more importantly, her steadfastness. This would be a trait that was manifest in him as well (though not always to his benefit). For her, it was an obvious choice; in fact, the *only* choice. But even then, certainly not an *easy* choice.

One can imagine the impact of such a decision, not just for her, but for her family; after all, here was Father Vincent, all those years later, recounting the story; for that matter, here

I am, one-hundred and seventy years later, her great-great-grandson, drawing strength from it, and doing the same. Her embrace of the gospel passage, "For what good is it to gain the whole world but lose your soul?" is legendary, and the essence of the living faith she breathed into the family.

Finally, *light came to her as she knelt,* he wrote. That mystical light was Goodness. That light was *Him.* She allowed that light entrance and, specially chosen for this witness, she, like that more glorious mother, gave her fiat. Remarkable.

✠

So, how should we walk with Father Vincent? Let's turn, first, to the mere act; and not that it is mere at all. The wonder of it is astounding, this ability to *move.* Yes, as Father Vincent remarked, *the wonder of the human foot.* He was good at moving those feet, and the physical act of walking with him was seen as an honor. One time, after a Sunday talk at the Catholic Evidence Guild, a young man asked if he could pay for a taxi ride back to the Priory for both of them, so he could hear more from the learned Friar. Father Vincent declined but invited him to walk back to the Priory with him instead. The young man recounted the experience:

> He walked me off my feet. I'm only half his age but he kept on at a steady pace, while I found it hard to keep up with him. Fr. McNabb urged me on and said I would find it easier if I talked, but he did most of the talking as I was out of breath after the first mile. He invited me to walk back with him the next Sunday, as he said I would find it easier with practice ... but I told him a bus was good enough for me![12]

Walking, for Father Vincent, was self-transport, and it was natural exercise. But as he was transfixed not on this life, but on the next, to walk with him would be to focus not on the physical act but on the spiritual. Like St. Dominic, it was said of Father Vincent that he spoke only to God or of God. To walk with him now would be to try to know God, through him, through his words and through his life. What needs to be remembered, above all, is that he was a preacher. Preachers profess truth, and preachers desire conversion. Nowhere are his intentions made more manifest than in his impending death.

On the tenth anniversary of Father Vincent's passing, Fr. Hilary Carpenter, O.P., Provincial of the English Dominicans, began his eulogy by telling the story not of Father Vincent's life, but of his wishes for his burial, which he saw as yet another opportunity to preach. I find it fitting to do so here, too. Fr. Carpenter writes:

> Knowing his end to be drawing near—it was in fact the day before his death—Father Vincent McNabb was concerned to make certain provisions for his funeral. Calling one of the younger brethren to him, he said to him:
>
> "Dear father, I may well die tomorrow and there is a service I would ask of your charity. I don't want a shaped and polished coffin such as they provide, nor should I like to have a brass factory-made cross on it nor be labelled with a brass label. I want an ordinary box made of the same sort of wood as this floor." He pointed with a smile to the common deal floor, uneven and knotted, which he had swept day by day with his bare hand, a floor such as had been his only bed for forty years and more.
>
> "You will want some measurements, of course; go and get a tape and measure me now; leave a bit extra length for me to stretch and plenty of room for the shoulders. When I am in the box and have been taken down to the church, bring away the lid and get out your brushes and black pigment and paint a cross on it, a good big one. Then you will want the inscription; I will dictate it to you: 'Ven. et Adm. R.P.F. Vincentius McNabb, O.P., S.T.M., Natus 8 Iulii 1868, Professus 28 Nov. 1886. Mortuus'—I don't know the date probably tomorrow, but anyway, '1943 Londini.' Now after that I want you to put a Greek inscription.
>
> Κύριε, *πάντα σὺ οἶδας, σὺ γινώσκεις ὅτι φιλῶ σε.*
>
> "They are the words of my text, 'Lord, thou knowest all things, thou knowest that I love thee.'
>
> "Then, after the *Requiem* and the *Libera*, to Kensal Green. I don't wish to be taken there in a glass-house. Borrow the builder's lorry and let down the sides. Put me

> on it, and let the two acolytes sit one on either side with their candles. (Don't light the candles; they will only get blown out.) Have the boy with the processional cross with his back to the driver's cab, and let me be driven to Kensal Green like that. Of course, I know that some people will say: 'That's McNabb and his tomfoolery, McNabb and his publicity, showing off.' But it isn't that, my dear Father, it isn't that. All my life I have preached and when I am no longer alive I shall still preach. *I shall preach even with my dead body* ... Now of course I realise I have a vow of obedience and you will need the Prior's permission to do all this."[13]

The prior did, in fact, grant permission, to at least some of it. As his niece, Sr. Mary Magdalene, O.P., noted,

> Crowds of people, young and old, rich and poor, flocked to see him and pray, and to touch him with their rosaries, crucifixes or pictures ... the Church was packed, the sanctuary full; priests, a bishop, two Monsignori, and four canons. Five benches in the middle of the church were full with clergy ... the coffin was carried by nine Knights of the Blessed Sacrament ... A great number of people crowded the road near the church and many who had been at Requiem hurried onto buses for Kensal Green [to witness the burial].[14]

And E. A. Siderman noted, "Obituary notices in newspapers and periodicals of all shades of political and religious opinion testified to his untiring work for social reform over the years, made mention of his walking about London, and his Dominican habit." But perhaps most poignantly, Siderman also recounted, "A few weeks after his death, one well-known speaker of the Guild said, 'Soon, we will not be praying *for* him, we will be praying *to* him.'"[15]

✠

I do pray to him. Or not *to* him, *per se*, but to him *for* his intercession. I have always felt a connection to this priest and uncle I never knew, who died just twenty-five years before my birth. He was very close to my great-grandfather, Patrick, who emigrated to Boston around 1900 and spawned a New World branch of the McNabbs of Portaferry, County Down. Patrick died in 1960, just eight years before I was born. I hold tight to that closeness of time, and to this closeness of relation, because it helps me feel closer to Father Vincent. Father Vincent can seem, like to many of those Londoners who ogled this man "from a previous century," *distant*; distant in time and place, but, perhaps more than anything, in holiness.

If ever I was given an inkling of what he was like, it was through his niece, Sr. Eleanor McNabb, my grandfather's sister. Unlike the Dominican vocations Father Vincent inspired in my family (there are seven of them—including myself, a Lay Dominican—and counting), Sr. Eleanor was a Daughter of Charity and exuded a beautiful, loving, caring, holy, joyful benevolence. She was joy, pure joy. And she was beloved. I would occasionally, in my teens, receive from her an encouraging note, an offer to send me a rosary if I needed one, or just mention of her prayers for me. And on those occasions when I would see her, she had that quality of attention that made me feel I was the most important person in the world by the way she smiled at me, the questions she asked. Father Vincent said many times how much he loved *people*. In a letter to E. A. Siderman, he admits, "all my life long I have loved persons more than places, even the most beautiful places. Indeed, I love people so much and I am sorry to be a pain to them that I find myself almost avoiding them."[16]

In Sr. Eleanor's smile and in her questions was that uncommon quality of true love of neighbor. When I was younger and in Sr. Eleanor's presence, I remember thinking this was what Father Vincent must have been like. Not all religious are this way, of course, but *she* was, and somehow, through her, I knew *he* was. I simply *knew*. And there she was—and, in a way, *he* was—right there before me.

This makes sense, of course. There are commonalities to holiness. That first and greatest commonality would be, in fact, love.

In love there is joy, which Father Vincent was known to exude. His lack of desire for material possessions was certainly one reason for his lightheartedness. In his cell were a bed (which he never slept in), a desk (which he only stood at), and three books (the Bible, the *Summa,* and the Constitution of the Dominican Order). He loved people, and no one was merrier or more lighthearted than he in the company of his brethren.[17]

From the platform of the Catholic Evidence Guild, where he preached for decades, he would often say how fortunate he considered himself, to be able to spend his time there, weekly, with them, with *people.* Given his understanding of the nature and meaning of our existence, people were important to him. And given his own modest upbringing, closest to his heart were common people. It gave him great pleasure to be among them.

Even with death imminent, he was intentional about maintaining his joy. When the throat cancer that would bring about his death prevented him from swallowing, he remarked to his niece,

> I am in no pain. But swallowing has now become a fine art requiring a master's special touch. Moreover, I smile and smile; because God wants me to smile and it does me good. *"Ridebit in die novissimo"* ["he will laugh on the last day"] is my slogan. Moreover, I don't want to qualify as a wet blanket![18]

This joy, to which he was naturally disposed, was encouraged as part of his vocation, and this suited him just fine. In his reminiscences of his time as a Novice in the Order, he writes:

> I was immensely surprised and delighted when I became a Dominican to find that sadness was never considered to be one of the products of the religious life. Sometimes you had to afflict yourself with bodily austerities but if you hadn't joy, out you went! Long faces were not considered outward and visible signs of sanctity.[19]

✠

Large families are inclined toward joy. This was certainly true of the McNabb eleven, where, if anyone was feeling down at the mouth was reminded, "Cheer up; you'll soon be dead!"[20] It is humorous—and true—but it also speaks to the presence of faith in a Catholic family, where death, not in its morbidity, but in its reality, should never be far from our minds.

That joy that my great-aunt, Sr. Eleanor, shared with Father Vincent, is a fruit of family. When Ann Shields returned home to Ireland from New York, she soon met her husband to be, James McNabb. As Father Vincent remarks, "Naturally enough the incidents that led to my mother giving her hand to a young captain of no great prospects were a romance not communicated to their children. But I think that the deep, life-long love between them was love at first sight."[21] He goes on to say, "It is difficult to describe the relation of my mother to my father except by calling it simply the sacramental relation between a wife and her husband."[22]

In a sacramental relation there will be holiness. When holiness is present, love is surely found. In holiness and love, faith is imparted almost as in the D.N.A. The fruits of this marriage were many, not the least of which were the eleven, where my great-grandfather, Patrick, was the eighth, and Joseph (as Father Vincent was named by his parents), or Joe, as he was called by his siblings his entire life, was tenth. His name saint would be so significant for him, and his mother, throughout his entire life. He remarks:

> The Christian name I bear, Joseph, is for me a daily reminder of my mother's hold on God, and the friends of God. Shortly before I was born, in 1868, a mission was given by some Passionist Fathers in the parish church, St. Patrick's, Portaferry. The effects of this mission are still traceable in the parish after seventy years; they were always traceable in my mother's life. Especial admiration and reverence were given to one of the fathers, named Fr. Joseph. Out of gratitude to him and still more out of reverence for God's Foster-father, St. Joseph [at St. Patrick's church, in front of the statue of St. Joseph] ... She lifted me up in her hands, holding me on high as an offering. Her own account of her offertory prayers was: "I said to St. Joseph, 'Here he is—take him—and do what you like with him.'"[23]

And St. Joseph certainly did a lot with him. Much more will be said about the impact and influence of St. Joseph on both Father Vincent and his mother, but unsurprisingly, the names Joseph, and Vincent, are now prominent names in my family. Vincent started as Joseph, and so those two names have carried on, sometimes even together, as Vincent Joseph, or even Joseph Vincent. Father Vincent's brother, Laurence, had a son named Vincent, and a daughter named Josephine. My grandfather was Joseph Vincent, and so was my uncle. My grandfather also had a brother, Vincent, who died in babyhood. My father is Thomas Joseph, and so is my brother. Wanting to spread the goodness, my older son is Luke Vincent, and my younger son is Leo Joseph.

But more impressively, the naming of boys after Father Vincent extends well beyond the family. His first assignment as prior of a Dominican community and parish was at Leicester, where there would ensue an astonishing "number of boys who were given the name Vincent at baptism, three of whom later became priests."[24] One of those actually thought his name, early on, was not just Vincent, but "Vincent McNabb" because of the number of times his family had mentioned that name. Incredibly, "Years later, the little boy who claimed to be Vincent McNabb was ordained a priest by Cardinal Bourne, and it was Father McNabb's letter that was waiting for him at the Cathedral to welcome him to the priesthood and to ask his blessing."[25] And there were at least two others of note. The first of these was even a non-Catholic. Father Vincent's niece, Eleanor McNabb, writes:

> In 1938 when the persecution of Catholics in Edinburgh was at its height Uncle Vincent went there to give a lecture of the Back to the Land movement. He walked as usual through the streets in his habit. To his delight he found that the Chairman, who was a Presbyterian clergyman, also one of eleven children, was accompanied on the platform by a Presbyterian layman who had christened one of his children "Vincent McNabb."[26]

But perhaps the most touching was the story, told by Father

Vincent directly to his biographer, of the brave and steadfast young pregnant woman who was told there would be a complication with her impending delivery and she may not survive, and her baby was at risk as well. She refused an abortion despite the doctor's recommendation and even her husband's protests. Fr. Valentine recounts the conversation:

> "But what's going to happen to me and the kids?" [said the husband.]
>
> "Look here, Dad,' she said, 'much as I love you all, don't you think God will bless you if I refuse to offend him?"
>
> "But hang it all! You've got another twenty or thirty years in front of you. You may have other children."
>
> "And the child? What of it?" asked the woman. "Won't it have much longer than me to live, and have kids of its own? In any case, I don't care what happens to me so long as nothing happens to my baby."
>
> When Father Vincent had told me this he suddenly took a step towards me. 'Now what do you think of that, Father?' he asked, very proud and very grim.
>
> "She was a heroine," I said.
>
> "Heroine!' he almost shouted. Then his face relaxed and he gave me that smile of his.
>
> "Perhaps you are right," he added. "Every good Catholic has to be something of a hero these days. I went to see her yesterday. She has been delivered of a bonny boy," he said rather shyly.
>
> "And what of the mother?" I asked.
>
> "She had a very bad time, but she's doing nicely, thank God."
>
> But still, he looked a bit embarrassed.
>
> "The nurse told me they are thinking of calling it Vincent," he murmured, as if talking to himself. Then he burst out laughing, "Poor devil!"[27]

✠

There is something in that exchange that would be a recurring theme for Father Vincent, the concept of Christian heroism. He knew, and thus taught, that all of one's actions are to be seen in the light of one's salvation. The concept of heroic virtue—one attribute by which saints are evaluated—dictates that in a given situation, one would have to display an inordinate amount of virtue—an heroic amount—to righteously prevail. We are weak, and so often *not* heroic. We succumb. We sin. Recognizing this, the environments we create for ourselves should be conducive to our only needing to routinely exhibit "regular" virtue. Think of someone with a gambling addiction walking into a casino in Las Vegas, or an alcoholic walking into a bar. That young mother, faced with a situation that most people would have rationalized, chose the more difficult route, the one she felt aligned with God's word and God's will. Most would have succumbed. Perhaps even understandably so. She emerged a hero.

At the time, one of Father Vincent's causes was to urge the poor masses, who had flocked to the cities to take up jobs in factories and the like, to "flee to the fields." He decried men and women leaving the countryside to work in often degrading circumstances and live in flats. There was an essential incongruence. His contention was there was no possibility, with wages and rents what they were, for the average working man to have a family and still be called "responsible" by his peers.

As Siderman recounts Father Vincent preaching from the platform:

> "Flats. Flats. Flats. That's the proper name for them," he said derisively. "They are not homes—they cannot be a proper home for a family; they are just packing-cases to pack people into."
>
> He expressed his opinion that the building of flats for people to live in would inevitably cause a decrease in the number of children born, because owing to the restriction of space and the lack of a garden for children to play in, parents would be forced to decide against having children.
>
> And then he added grimly, "They are led into the practice of birth control, or abortion, which is plain murder."[28]

Siderman leaves off with the humorous but poignant remark from Father Vincent:

> "People used to live in homes, now they live in flats. You know what is meant by the phrase 'I am going home.'—Can you imagine anyone saying, 'I am going flat?'"[29]

Sadly, the corruption of our culture and society is even more profound today and extends well beyond how we make our living. More will be said about that in the coming pages. In so many aspects of our lives, heroic virtue is required to simply get through a day without defilement. Just turn on the television to see what passes as "family" entertainment. My children have cell phones, often portals to ungodliness. I know that pornography floods their way. We do our best to limit that, actively encouraging virtue, but there is so much beyond our control. We are torn between limiting these, and other occasions and teaching them to avoid—even if heroically—what they may lead to. It is our policy to engage the world to transform it, not avoid it. It is difficult to determine where that line is. It is hard not to wonder if we are making the right choices in our efforts to protect them in our determination to live "in the world." In this, I ask, *Father Vincent, Pray for us!*

BUT FORTITUDE. Returning to the character of Ann; she was bedrock and strength and devotion. She trusted. All of us walking through our times today can draw from her resolve. As Father Vincent recounts:

> "When my mother was still suckling her fourth child, she determined to go with my father in a little vessel, the *Elizabeth,* round Cape Horn to Callao [the voyage would take two years.] When the ship arrived at New Zealand, it was evident my mother was about to give birth. My father, under a stern sense of duty, said to the expectant mother: "Ann, don't you think you had better stay here in New Zealand instead of risking the voyage to Callao? I can pick you up on the way back."
>
> "No, James," she said, "I will go with you. God will provide."
>
> The first mate used to describe what happened in his own way: "Well," he would say, "I don't believe in God or the Devil. But the day that child was born was a miracle. There had been storms for weeks before; there were storms for weeks after. But the day the child was born, the Pacific was as calm as a mill pond!"
>
> My readers can imagine all that went to my mother's emphatic, "God will provide"—when they are told that on the little ship there was no doctor but my father and no woman other than my mother.[30]

Years later, when Father Vincent was recounting the story to a group of Socialist and Communist mothers who had come to listen to him give the Catholic view of birth control, he told them,

> quietly, but perhaps a little proudly, of this heroism of a mid-Victorian mother. I hardly know why I alluded to the wonderful feat performed by a young woman flying alone and in record time to Australia. Then I added: I do not wish to belittle the courage of this young air-woman. Hers was a great feat. But I think my mother's was no less great.
>
> Almost before I had finished saying this . . . I was startled by a burst of spontaneous applause. I bowed my head in silence for a spell, because I recognized in the spontaneous applause of these yet unspoiled mothers a group of women who were honouring woman's redemptive heroism of child-birth.[31]

In this last anecdote, in addition to the obvious strength of Ann McNabb, Father Vincent gives us just a glimpse of one of the topics, birth control, that he, as a preacher and a priest, sought to combat in his ministry of souls.

✠

We tend to think of birth control as a modern problem. In the following piece, Father Vincent refers to birth control as "lust uncontrol." And as Chesterton famously called it, "No birth, and No control." Father Vincent's sister-in-law, Maud McNabb, recounts the following:

> Father Vincent's visit to us were always a great joy. My husband and Father Vincent, even as boys, always had great admiration for each other. This continued all through life, and my husband's death was a great sorrow to him. During Fr. Vincent's visits he was always ready for an argument or deep discussions with my husband or for a game with children. One discussion I remember was on birth control. This was the time when some thought this subject should not be spoken about in public. Uncle Vincent differed. But I well remember him pushing back his chair and saying to my husband: "If my Superiors think the matter should not be spoken about," or words to that effect, "well that ends it, this applies to any of my opinions."[32]

Speak about it, he did. One such instance was a published piece in the American Catholic magazine, *Commonweal*, the oldest independent Roman Catholic journal of opinion in the country, publishing for nearly a hundred years up to the present day. Father Vincent was invited to contribute a piece to its pages in 1925. In yet another sign-of-the-times, the straightforwardness of this contribution would now no longer be acceptable to the editors at that very same magazine, *Commonweal*. They would be scandalized and embarrassed to print such a thing. More about that at the end of his contribution. Here is "Modern Marriage—Its Problems," with the sub-title, "The Catholic Church and Birth Control" (note: neo-Malthusianism is the advocacy of population control):

> What has the Roman Catholic Church to say on the matters most discussed at present concerning the married state? Let us offer first-aid to thinking on a subject where thinking has become entangled. The Church does not condemn marriage. The Church exalts marriage by giving it the name and dignity of a great sacrament. But the Church has no authority to approve anything masquerading as marriage, whether this thing is concubinage or adultery.
>
> The Church does not condemn birth-control. Indeed, by its teaching on virginal and conjugal chastity it has exercised such an effective birth-control that Malthus's gloomy prophecies were never fulfilled. But the Church has no authority to approve anything merely masquerading as birth-control, when this thing is called lust un-control.
>
> If a man and a woman wish to have the sacrament of marriage, they can have it on certain conditions. If they do not wish to have the sacrament, they need not have it. The conditions of a Christian marriage are that the marriage act shall be used for begetting children. If the man and woman intend to seek sterile venereal satisfaction with the help of chemical or mechanical appliances, this is not marriage. It is a form of harlotry, which keeps the old Christian name of marriage.
>
> Moreover, this neo-Malthusian union is not the marriage act; but a scientific form of mutual self-abuse. This is the plain English, the common sense of it.
>
> The Church is accused of claiming autocratic power in this matter of neo-Malthusian birth-control. But, quite on the contrary, the Church professes that it has no power.
>
> As to divorce, it says: "If a man and a woman are truly married we have no power to allow the marriage to be

broken." As to neo-Malthusianism, it says: "If a man and a woman are truly married, we have no power to allow the marriage act to be broken."

But what the Church says it has no power or authority to do the State and individuals claim the power to do. Thus, the State claims to have the power and authority to break marriage by divorce; individuals claim to have the power to break the marriage act by neo-Malthusian self-abuse.

In disclaiming this power and authority to allow these crimes against marriage, the Church is acting on a basis, not of sentimentality, but of consistent reasoning. It must be remembered that this matter of marriage and neo-Malthusianism is not the only matter submitted to the Church's judgment. Other matters affected by like principles are also submitted to ethical judgment of the Church. A false decision on this matter, even if given in the interest of a hard case, would imperil the whole of morality.

Thus, if by allowing neo-Malthusianism the Church allowed masturbation within marriage, it could not forbid it outside marriage. Or, again, if child-birth being dangerous and husband was allowed to procure venereal satisfaction by artificial means with his wife, it would be impossible to condemn him for seeking the same satisfaction by natural means with a woman who was not his wife. Indeed, these conclusions are not speculative, but actual. We are asked, in the name of hard cases, to sanction parenthood without wedlock. We are even asked, in the name of hygiene, to allow puberty to be a right to harlotry. And at a recent conference on the sex relations, a clergyman asked whether the time had not come for reconsidering the arguments against sodomy.

Another application of a false principle may be of even greater help towards sound thinking. Almost the only argument, and certainly the main argument used when propagating neo-Malthusianism amongst the poor, is the poverty which makes it necessary to limit the family. Neo-Malthusianism is confessed to be an evil; yet it is claimed to be the lesser of two evils.

But from these principles some conclusions result which are not likely to please the wealthy folk who propagate neo-Malthusianism amongst the poor. If the Church approves neo-Malthusianism on this economic plea of

> the lesser of two evils, how can it disapprove of theft on the same plea? A husband may say: "My wages are too small to have another child, but my wife and I hate these nasty neo-Malthusian devices. Now, as I am a clerk, I can quite easily steal two pounds a week. I feel this is the lesser of two evils. I confess it is an evil to steal. But it is a greater evil not to get a family wage. And I wish you to approve what I do."
>
> The Church which claimed authority to approve neo-Mathusianism would have no authority to disapprove of theft. For this reason, the Church rests her action on the principle—non possumus. We cannot.

In this piece, Father Vincent wrote, "The Church does not condemn birth-control." At the time this was written, this was true. His point, which remains true, is that the Church does not *not* have a position, but birth control could *never be assented to* if one follows the Faith, and so the Church, from its existence has condemned the practice *a priori.* The gory freight-train of sexual liberalism necessitated, however, four decades later, Pope Paul VI to bravely issue the encyclical letter, *Humanae Vitae,* explicitly forbidding the use of birth control. From the time of the issuance of the letter, *Commonweal* has attempted in its pages, even up to the present day, to untie that knot, citing the majority of Catholics who use birth control and other supposed justifications. I will just briefly note his comment about the clergyman asking, "whether the time had not come for reconsidering the arguments against sodomy." This, of course, has great relevance today, and it is important to see that our current miasma has been decades (some would say, centuries) in the making. My question: was Father Vincent wrong in his assessment? The answer is either Yes or No, or are things, as the world tells us today, um, *complicated.*

✠

Father Vincent's intellect was obvious, and though he was brilliant, he never flaunted his intelligence or learning. It was part of his appeal, and what made him so successful. As Siderman noted,

> Always lucid, he made the most difficult theological subjects understandable; as was the case with controversial moral and social problems. He spoke in a language people could understand and never used a long or difficult word if he could use an easier or simpler expression. He was never dull or dry in either sermons or lectures, but always most interesting, with flashes of subtle wit, with many amusing illustrations and expressive gestures. His was not a "Pulpit" voice. It was friendly, conversational, almost intimate in tone and expression, taking his listener into his confidence.[33]

He was a learner, and this was evident from an early age. He attended the prestigious St. Malachy's College (grammar and high school) in Belfast. At age fourteen, his father was given an on-land commission, and the family moved to Newcastle-on-Tyne, England. The Master at the school was very sorry to see him go, but it wasn't long before young Joe would return. My great-grandfather tells the story that Joe

> was so far ahead of the other boys in the class [at his new school, St. Cuthbert's] that he walked away with practically all the prizes at the end of the school year. This compelled the school authorities to inform my mother that as they could not form a class of boys of Joe's mental caliber, they had decided not to accept him for another term. It was for this reason he returned to St. Malachy's at Belfast, where [as a boarder] he finished his secular education.[34]

He remained a learner his entire life. Indeed, one of the four pillars of Dominican life is Study. Later in life, he wrote, "There is hardly a day when I have not studied, even if only for a few moments."[35]

After he was raised to the priesthood in 1891, he was sent to Louvain in Belgium where he earned his Licentiate in Sacred Theology, which enabled him to teach. He went on to teach his brethren as a professor of philosophy and sacred theology. He taught conferences at Oxford. He was later elected prior of the House of Studies, where he was Regent, and Professor of Dogmatic Theology and Social Science. In 1916, he was awarded the highest academic distinction within the

Order, Master of Sacred Theology, which required passing the *Ad Gradus* examination and having taught for twelve years. Though he was learned, or perhaps because of it, he had this to say about what was becoming of education: "There are many Catholics ... priests, teachers and parents, who seem to regard the purpose of education as a means of what is called 'getting on in the world.'"[36]

My wife and I are hardly what one would call intellectual, but we do place an emphasis on education for our children. Our older son is in the process of applying to colleges. This is both exciting, because he is growing up and moving on, and depressing, for the very same reason. And overwhelming, because we are a family of six and the cost of this education is absurd and we cannot possibly pay what will be asked of him and his siblings and so there will be, potentially, a mountain of debt. And disheartening, because of just what Father Vincent said regarding "getting on in the world," and the foolishness of the mostly inauthentic resume burnishing to get into "elite" colleges in the first place. And concerning, because of the unwelcome and unrooted environment at most colleges and universities today, even "Catholic" ones. And worrisome, because my son is a fighter and has quite an intellect, and he doesn't roll over. He has been in difficult situations in high school classrooms because of that; though this, actually, is to his great credit. Father Vincent, I am sure, would be proud of his hewing to Truth, being able to explain it, and not backing down. But concerning, again, because of the lack of authenticity of the education, and because of the "what is it going to get me" mentality, which is somewhat understandable given the outrageous cost rendering the experience, out of necessity, a cost-benefit equation. And finally, what are one's prospects in the current workplace, especially in larger corporations which have become less about the reason they exist and more about pushing social agendas? What becomes of us at the Bank we work for should we decline the Rainbow Flag pen holder? That we are talking with our children about which professions to enter and not enter relating to a prediction about future requirements to bow to a secular god says a lot about where we are. It can be daunting.

We want our children to *learn,* because in rightly rooted learning there is the proper use of God's gifts, and in learning, whether it is algebra or dogmatic theology, a glimpse of Him, or a whole lot more, can be discovered.

✠

In this regard, we sometimes pray *A Student's Prayer,* composed by Father Vincent's hero, the great Dominican, St. Thomas Aquinas:

> Come, Holy Spirit, Divine Creator, true source of light and fountain of wisdom! Pour forth your brilliance upon my dense intellect, dissipate the darkness which covers me, that of sin and of ignorance. Grant me a penetrating mind to understand, a retentive memory, method and ease in learning, the lucidity to comprehend, and abundant grace in expressing myself. Guide the beginning of my work, direct its progress, and bring it to successful completion. This I ask through Jesus Christ, true God and true man, living and reigning with You and the Father, forever and ever. Amen.

✠

Unsurprisingly, Father Vincent displayed an uncommon holiness from an early age. One memory from my great-grandfather speaks to this awareness in young Joe. And it also speaks to the aforementioned concern for the disposition of his soul, which was a lifelong struggle for him. He was prone to scrupulosity as a young man, and while he advanced beyond that at the direction of a priest in the confessional, his great awareness of human frailty and God's goodness and the Four Last Things was never far from his mind—for himself, and for others.

But as for my great-grandfather's story. The family moved into a new house and he and Joe shared a small bedroom. Before long, Joe "erected a small altar in the corner of the room, before which we said our morning and night prayers … I would rise from my knees and dress for bed, but he would remain on his knees with his head bowed and resting on his two hands."

This carried on night after night, until eventually Patrick asked him, "what on earth has been keeping you on your knees after night prayers?"

> Then in a voice trembling with emotion, he reluctantly divulged his secret, "Patrick," he said, "some time ago I made Almighty God a promise. I promised that every night before I went to bed I would try to put myself in that frame of mind in which I would like to be if He called me to Judgment before the morning."
>
> Needless to say, never after that did I make any further comment on his prayerfulness.[37]

But to dispel the notion that all was simple piety in their home, the McNabb boys were known to be a rowdy lot. As my great-grandfather told Father Vincent's biographer,

> We McNabb boys were a gang of daredevils and always getting into trouble, as my mother would tell you if she was alive. The stout leather strap she always carried with her was frequently called upon to administer well-deserved punishments.

He did add, though: "Nevertheless, I can never recall seeing Joe punished in this way for a misdemeanor of any kind."[38]

The "strap" comment made me laugh. I don't know if this is a term used outside my family, but "the strap" made its way down to my generation, and it was often threatened—and occasionally, employed—when I was growing up. Another legacy of the great Ann McNabb. Unlike Joe, though, I was not immune to misdemeanors.

TODAY, in the Church we often hear the phrase "accompaniment," which would be a form of "walking with." The concept, of course, is deeply Christian. "Accompanying" our neighbor is to walk with him in his struggles; in a word, to *love* him, and loving our neighbor is one of the two greatest Commandments. Might it be said, though, that the manner in which we are being encouraged to walk with our neighbor today is less than straight?

The level of ambiguity in just how we are to accompany those in need, particularly relating to hot-button issues relating to sexual morality, is high. Much is written of Father Vincent's exploits as a preacher, but one thing is certain, he accompanied many in a truly Christian way, mostly outside of the public eye, and always with decided clarity. Siderman writes of one such account:

> Of all the practical acts of mercy and love with which his life abounded, it would be quite impossible to write, but this narrative will give the reader some idea of the trouble he would go to (though he would never have admitted it to be a trouble) to succor those in distress. The young daughter of a parishioner of his had been taken away to a fever hospital and the mother, in great distress and anxiety for her child, confided her fears to Father Vincent. He comforted her as best he could and promised he would call and see the child and report her condition on his return. Having received the necessary permission, he [walked to] the Fever hospital, a distance of five miles, was clad in a sterilized gown and went into the suffering

> girl. He stayed some time, and before leaving, presented her with a rosary. Then back to the mother he went with his report. He made those visits and reports frequently. Then soon after the girl left hospital, her brother and sister were also stricken with fever and removed to the same hospital. Father Vincent recommenced his long journeys to and from the hospital, and his visits of comfort to the distracted mother. The measure of his love and compassion will be better understood, when it is mentioned that these visits extended to a period of nearly twelve months.[39]

This example of accompaniment—of walking with (and in this case, *to*)—is inspiring, particularly given how truly busy and in demand he was as a priest.

This example relates to corporal works, but there is a no less spiritual element to this manner of accompaniment. Today, the elements of accompaniment that are most urged, it seems, are also the most controversial; these relate to issues of sexual morality. But how does one *accompany* without giving assent to sin?

There is a perception in some corners that a "rigid" orthodoxy seeks to undermine the current pope and his approach. What Father Vincent would say about these moral issues today is plain, but one thing is not, and that is his respect for authority and for obedience, and particularly with regard to the pope. He had this to say when asked by a questioner at the Catholic Evidence Guild:

> "What do you think of this present Pope [Pius XI]?"
>
> "What exactly do you mean?" asked Father Vincent. "Do you mean: Do I like him?"
>
> "Yes."
>
> "Well! It's a question I don't know how to answer: it has never occurred to me. Do you have to like the Boss? We're not asked to like the Pope: that doesn't matter much, as long as we *obey* him."[40]

✠

In terms of obedience, Father Vincent learned respect for authority from his parents—his father was a sea captain and surely instilled in him the need for recognition of a chain of command, and his mother had a natural deference—this was good training for the required obedience of his Dominican life. His relishing intellectual discourse (or argumentativeness, as some have asserted) rendered him an effective debater, and so holding his tongue required no small effort. He would find himself in hot water a number of times, but regarding the pope, Father Vincent writes this:

> Though I cannot recall one instance of my father or mother questioning an action or word of the head priest, the Pope, yet I can recall the phrase with which their true Catholic attitude towards the Pope was summed up: "We take our religion from Rome; not our politics." But the phrase was not of their coining. It came from the head of the great Catholic whose heart, by his own will, was buried in Rome—Daniel O'Connell.[41]

Daniel O'Connell was the revered Irish statesman who worked hard for freedoms and representation for Irish Catholics. Father Vincent's reference to O'Connell is, oddly enough, one of the rare times he mentions the struggles of the Irish. As Siderman notes, Father Vincent was sometimes taken to task by countrymen who thought he should be more outspoken. To be sure, and particularly because he was an Ulsterman, the repression of Irish Catholics in his native land—and even in his adopted land—could not have sat well with him. Fr. Bernard Delany, O.P., who served as Prior Provincial of the English Dominicans in the 1930s and thus knew Fr. Vincent quite well, wrote:

> Father Vincent never lost his love for Ireland: he wept for her sorrows. He wrote of the social ills that made Ireland bleed. In an essay, "The Voice of the Irish", with all the poetry of a romantic soul, and the nostalgia of the exiled Gael, he describes the cry of the Irish as, "the sob of my blood-kindred whom years of exile have not torn from my heart.[42]

But he never allowed Ireland's struggles to discolor his love for the English. He would often say, "I love Ireland as a mother, and England as a wife."

✠

Yes, Father Vincent loved England. He loved in many ways. One deep love was for his priestly vocation. And he knew his vocation *required* love. From the platform of the Catholic Evidence Guild one Sunday, he said:

> Nowadays, most people are anxious to see what they can get, not what they can give. Many will be judged by their response to the Commandment, "Love Thy Neighbor." I come here to tell you these things because I love you, and want you to understand what is good for you. We priests do not often preach on these things as often as we should, but we know that if we do not love men, we should not preach to them; we should preach to ourselves. But, if we really love them, we need never be afraid to speak to them, for they will know it and welcome it.[43]

Priests are human. We have all met priests who are good at their job, who inspire, who approach their vocation with energy, who seek to grow in holiness and inspire their flock to grow in holiness, too. We also know priests who seem indifferent or wayward or even lazy (though I would imagine it is difficult being lazy these days, with all the responsibilities our priests have). One thing is certain, though, respect for the priesthood was required within his family. He writes:

> My mother's (and father's) reverence for the priesthood was but one flowering of their belief that Jesus Christ was God. If anyone in the family began to criticize a priest for his sermon or parish-work my mother would become instantly uneasy as if in pain. She would begin to move about the room saying in a pained voice: "Now, now … don't let us say anything against God's anointed!"[44]

He continues:

> Whatever this reverence of a Catholic mother for the Catholic priest appeared to those who did not share her faith, it was a faith compatible with and indeed built with a strong sense of human reality. Priests were not superhuman beings; they were, even in the Island of Saints, merely human beings with supernatural powers.

> Often enough, even in the Island of Saints, they asserted their humanity in a painful way.[45]

Being a priest today is a tremendous challenge and they need our prayers. In most places, particularly in the West, the lack of vocations has rendered the responsibilities overwhelming. Add to this the sex abuse scandals, the hostility toward Catholicism, their being natural "signs of contradiction," and the focus of criticism even from within the Church, and the stress can be understood. And there is a focus, now, on the nebulous concept of *clericalism*, which seems to be used as either an excuse, or a cudgel, depending on the wielder.

This reminds me of my time living in Ireland when, one night, while flipping through the channels on television, I stopped on a show where two priests and a moderator were on stage in front of an audience. I forget the topic, but the tone with which audience members were addressing the priests was shocking. I wondered, why the irreverence? I pictured myself in the audience defending the priests, who seemed to be there of their own accord to represent Church teaching. I remember how I thought I would start my comments, "I am just a Yank, but . . ." I know there are issues that escape me as an American. I know the ire was not directed at those priests personally, but at the priesthood. Maybe there is something to gripe about. I know there is a history of different types of abuse within the Irish church. Maybe I could be accused of "clericalism" which, again, seems to mean two exactly opposite things depending on who is giving a definition. I simply know of the exalted calling of these chosen sons. But priests are not the same thing as the Church. I guess it bears reflecting on Ann McNabb's wise words, "Often enough, [priests] asserted their humanity in a painful way."[46]

✠

From the time I was a child I held up the priestly vocation as the highest position a man could hold, exceeding that of surgeon or astronaut or even president. The supernatural aspect of the calling was what greatly impressed. A life dedicated to

God. It was—and is—so *mysterious*. The wearing of black. The solitude. The being separate, if you will, from society. I was never tempted, because I saw a vow of celibacy as the most difficult bullet point requirement any job description could ever have. I was a fool. I used to think it humorous to say to my friends, the only job I know I'm not called to is the priesthood. While as true as that is, I was, in that matter, and in so many others, just a boaster and a poseur.

I do not know if any of my children are being called to religious life, but I occasionally ask them to consider it. It is usually, if I am being honest, an afterthought, but something pricks me when I am asking them about their plans for the future, which I frequently do, directing them in one worldly way or another.

✠

But about Father Vincent and his "obsessiveness," as some have called it, regarding his soul's disposition. It would be a lifelong theme. Of his motive for entering religious life, he said, perhaps only half-kidding, "I don't want to go to Hell, I think I'll go to the Novitiate."[47]

His biographer makes the following assertion:

> Those who will persist in seeing him merely in the context if his exterior life—his social work, his ability as a controversialist, his agile and penetrating mind, and even his unusual insight into Theology will never understand how grievously he was troubled by the plight of his own soul in search of humility and a happy death.[48]

There is a fine line between scrupulosity and love and fear of God. He straddled that line. I believe his awareness, his closeness with the Lord was so profound, his love so great, his relationship so deep that, as his niece, Sr. Mary Magdalene wrote, "he derived [every motive for his actions] from the needs of his own soul in search of union with God."

The holier one becomes, the more attuned to sin one is. It was not showmanship that prompted him to drop to the floor to kiss the feet of someone he thought he offended, it was genuine regret, a profound recognition of the stain of impurity. The holier one becomes, the more one desires Him both for himself and for others. It was not self-love that powered him forth through his busy days, but his guided mission.

Was he born with this ache? Perhaps. I have often wondered why some people are more inclined toward the faith than others, even those growing up in the very same home. In Ephesians 2:8, it is written, "For by grace you have been saved through faith, and this is not from you; it is the gift of God." Was Father Vincent's strong faith *given* to him, or to anyone who is a solid and growing practitioner? How do we reconcile this? We see it even in families where the rearing is consistent and the faith is dutifully imparted by the parents, some of the children embrace it, others do not.

I am reminded of a scene in *The Brothers McMullen*, the acclaimed Irish-American movie about three brothers navigating life and faith, which addresses just such a dynamic. When the oldest brother, Jack, cheats on his wife, the youngest brother, Patrick, confronts him and asks him if he's not concerned about the disposition of his soul and what God may think of him. I won't repeat what Jack said about God, but Patrick's reaction (humorous in context) is utter astonishment, a jaw-dropping dumbfoundedness at his brother's response, his disregard for the state of his soul, of what his fate, by his own hand, may be. Patrick had it right, of course. But was he simply more inclined that way? Was Jack not given the same depth of faith? Was Jack just emotional in the moment or deviantly defiant? Did he not think it true that hell exists? Did he think he would have time to repent, but later?

Father Vincent was so desirous of spending eternity in the beatific vision, the words he instructed to be written on his coffin, "Lord, You know that I love thee," shout a reminder to God, a just-in-case. As if God did not know. But it was a begging, a pleading. I am certain he uttered these words frequently not, in the moment, as a reminder, but as a profession, as truth. And to this, I can relate.

✠

This leads me to consider a poem he wrote, *The One Whom Thou Lovest is Sick*. From the day I started writing, nearly twenty-five years ago, it has never been far. It is, clearly, a prayer, and indicative of his knowledge of his own weakness and his interior desire:

"Lord Jesus, the one whom Thou lovest is sick" (John 11:3)

The one whom Thou lovest is strayed.
I have lost Thee.
I cannot find Thee.
Find me.
Seek me.
I cannot find Thee.
I have lost my way.
Thou art the Way.
Find me, or I am utterly lost.
Thou lovest me.
I do not know if I love Thee;
but I know Thou lovest me.
I do not plead my love, but Thine.
I do not plead my strength, but Thine.
I do not plead my deed, but Thine.
The one whom Thou lovest is sick.
I dare not say:
The one who loves Thee is sick.
My sickness is that I do not love Thee.
That is the source of my sickness
  which is approaching death.
I am sinking.
Raise me.
Come to me upon the waters.
Lord Jesus, "the one whom Thou lovest is sick."

So, in this, in this appeal, in this devotion, in this recognition of his lowly state, and also in his desire to love both God and man, to explain to his God that his shortcomings are painful, are obvious, are a condition of his sickness, would He then, please, show mercy, heal him, forgive him, show him the way. It is the most profound appeal one can make.

This torment evades the realm of scrupulosity. It is simple recognition. It is desire. For Him. For what is to come.

Father Vincent would say, more than once, and perhaps with his mother's return to her native land in mind,

> I thank God Ireland is not a rich country. When a country becomes rich, its citizens usually become slack in the practice of their religion, and Ireland has kept the Faith when other countries have almost lost it.[49]

Ireland today, unfortunately for the Faith, is rich. Maybe even filthy rich. This is tragic. What has set the Irish apart for centuries has dissolved in a mere few generations. One cannot blame a people for seeking material gain, but there has been a direct, and inverse, relationship between Ireland's rising G.D.P. and its citizens' plummeting faith. Dissatisfaction with the traditional power of the clergy alongside various abuses had been brewing for some time previous to economic prospects looking up, of course. The opportunity to partake of the growing wealth addressed collective self-esteem issues relating to wealth relative to Western European neighbors, and many surged ahead without much looking back. Today, Ireland is not much different than the rest, and that is, indeed, unfortunate. Its two greatest exports had always been people (including many priests) and the Faith. Today, the number of vocations in the country cannot support the number of priests needed domestically, much less for export.

This 2020 headline in *The Economist* summarizes the present situation: "The Liberalisation of Ireland: How Ireland stopped being one of the most devout, socially conservative places in Europe." Mass attendance has fallen dramatically, marriage has been redefined and, seeking to put an end to the faith once and for all, teachers in Catholic schools are being targeted for simply teaching the faith, and there is even talk of the nationalization of Catholic schools, which would be the decided death-blow, effectively taking out faith at its roots. The former president, Mary McAleese, has advocated eliminating parents' rights to baptize their children, stating by doing so they are "infant conscripts who are held to lifelong obligations of obedience." The illogicality. The audacity. Shocking. Father Vincent would hardly recognize his native land.

Of the many signs of Ireland's moral decline, perhaps the saddest, yet most symbolic, is the recent passage of legislation making it possible to obtain an abortion in the country. In case there is any doubt as to the provenance of this evil, one need look no further than the Government's own official tally of the number of abortions performed that first year. The number? 6,666.[50]

✠

I am not an academic who can fully diagnose the historical context of faith, economics, and other contributing factors to the present situation in Ireland, but I am human and can see plain enough the result. I do have a personal connection to Ireland, through my heritage, and through personal history and the experience of having lived in Dublin, where I spent a good bit of time walking. Father Vincent's hand touched me even there—of course, at the end of a long walk. Here, briefly, is part of that story.[51]

> In 1998, I left my post-MBA job in international finance to become a writer. In my effort to be away from the eighty-hour work weeks and start afresh, I moved to Ireland for a time. I settled in Dublin, renting a "flat" [sorry, Father Vincent], just a few blocks from the Guinness brewery. This was the beginning of the emergence of the "new" Ireland from the "old" Ireland. At the time, the so-called "Celtic Tiger," a moniker given to the surprising Irish economy, was beginning to

roar. Dublin was becoming the "back office" of Europe. Multinational companies were moving parts of their operations to the country for the huge government tax breaks and the low-cost labor force of native English speakers. The many cranes on the city skyline gave an impression of a Mad Max post-apocalyptic reality. Or progress, depending on your perspective.

Though the decline had been progressing for decades, and mirrored, to a great extent, the overall decline of the Church in the West since the tumult of the 1960s, the situation in the late 1990s when I was there, was hardly what it is today. In any event, Ireland was, in many ways, one long walk for me. It was a different type of walk than those Father Vincent would take. Though there were certainly spiritual and mind-clearing benefits for him, my walks were decidedly less utilitarian. I was, and am, a creative ambler.

At the time, I was just learning how to put words on paper. I would write for several hours in the morning and then the rest of the day would be mine. I filled these hours with walking and reading. I had not been a great reader to that point. There was so much I didn't know, so many writers I *wanted* to know, so many works I felt I *needed* to know. There was the adage, "One can't write if one hasn't read." I hadn't read, and I was intent on writing. So I read. And I read and I read, filling my apartment with books from local bookstores now long-gone. My selections were all over the board, from Catholic writers Graham Greene and Flannery O'Connor to the whacked-out journalist Hunter Thompson and the beatnik William Burroughs. From Ernest Hemingway to Raymond Carver to Franz Kafka and beyond. It was reading, but it was also study. I was seeking answers, foremost among them, "How do you actually *do* this?"

Walking aided my education. I exulted in my loneliness, in my deep thought, in my prayer, in the words I was putting on paper, in the words of others I was reading, but perhaps most of all, in my meandering. My meandering took many forms, but it was that of foot that was most dear. Over the course of those months I walked, and I walked, and I walked, quite literally, hundreds and hundreds of miles throughout the city of Dublin, most of them beneath that beautifully inspiring, doleful gray sky.

That time spent walking was a time of prayer for me; not always explicit, word-based prayer, but a sort-of manifested exultant thankfulness. So few of us at such a young age are afforded the luxury I had; the luxury of time. I had nowhere I needed to go, nowhere I needed to be, and the funds to support myself. At times, I would go days without speaking to another human being. I would write in the morning and then be off; from the hum of the city-centre and the weighty darkness of its soot-coated buildings, to weed-addled lanes in outer districts and so much in between. From the expanse of the impossibly green Phoenix Park to the caged wildness of the garden in Merrion Square. From the quays on the River Liffey to the utilitarian access roads leading out of the city, I walked. I had my routes, but often I just ambled, discovering, marveling, lamenting, thinking, sighing, praying, seeking, asking. There were days when my thoughts were so occupying, or when something enticing seemed to be waiting just beyond reach, as if the answer would be around just one more corner, and then another, and another that I would walk so far I would find myself miles and miles from home; exhausted and unable to continue, I would sometimes take a taxi back [sorry, Father Vincent.]

And I would sit. In pubs, in coffee shops, on the benches at St. Stephen's Green, next to the Patrick Kavanagh statue on the Dublin Canal, on the stone steps in the Garden of Remembrance just up from Parnell Square, and in so many other places, spots I would return to time-and-again, or spots new. My favorite place was a bench in the little-known Iveagh Gardens, so rustic, so true. But it was a park bench in Mountjoy Square Park that I remember so fondly now.

On this particular day I was sitting and reading when an older man in his late-sixties or seventies, approached me and asked if I would like to join a Bible study group meeting that night. I don't remember what I said, except that it would have included the words, No, or, I don't think so. Whatever it was, my American accent came out and we got to talking about that and he asked me my name. When I told him, he looked at me and said, "You wouldn't be related to Father Vincent McNabb would you?" I told him I was.

The joy that overtook his face!

He yelled to a friend talking to someone a ways away, and beckoned him over. He could hardly get the words out fast enough, that I was related to Father Vincent, and I enjoyed a secondhand celebrity I had never experienced before.

Yes, Father Vincent was—and is—well-known, but I knew in my heart at that very moment that this was no coincidence. He was there. He was with me. I could feel it. And it wouldn't be the last time.

I was given a flyer by the old fellas with information about their prayer group and was asked, Would I, please, go to the next meeting? Indicative of my preference for developing my craft over developing my faith at the time, sadly, I never went.

✠

Whatever the state of my spiritual life at the time—and it was not bad; it was good, in fact, just immature—there was a path I was on that has brought me to today. While the path has been jagged, one of the benefits of spiritual maturity is acknowledgment of the need for trust in Him. We are called to this. Trust is faith and trust is belief. Trust is letting go. Trust is acknowledgment that our attempts to control everything are anxious and ego-driven and often futile. It is a deeply Christian concept.

Trust was a hallmark of Father Vincent's family. This, too, was inculcated by Ann McNabb, in ways big and small. Father Vincent writes of her standard—but not rote—response when asked how some challenging situation or other would unfold:

> If I were to set down all the kinds of happenings that begot my mother's characteristic phrase, "Thank God," or "Let us trust in God," most of my non-Catholic readers would look on her as a fatalist. We have seen how she faced the dangers of childbirth at sea with a complete, and as it turned out, justified trust in God.

But one small question he recounts from the time he was a child stands out for him. He asked: "Mother, what should we do if my father died?"

> To which she replied, instantly, in a manner "quietly and quieting," according to Father Vincent: "Don't worry child! God will provide."[52]

This echoes, of course, the words of the woman who steadfastly refused an abortion, who, responding to her husband's understandable concern for what would become of him and the children responded, "Don't you think God will provide?"

This level of spiritual engagement, enlightenment and understanding amongst these "ordinary" Catholics is inspiring. And though I know I need to trust, I still find myself worried and anxious, this father of four children in these troubled times. I am heartened, again, by Father Vincent's writing of his mother living St. Augustine's words that "she trusted as if everything depended on God; and acted as if everything depended on her."

Often, when I am in the midst of having forgotten what needs remembering regarding trust, my own efforts, and my self-focused self-reliance, the following will either pop into my head, or will be right there before me in the midafternoon prayer from the Liturgy of the Hours (Psalm 127).

> Unless the LORD build the house,
> they labor in vain who build.
> Unless the LORD guard the city,
> in vain does the guard keep watch.
> It is vain for you to rise early
> and put off your rest at night,
> To eat bread earned by hard toil—
> all this God gives to his beloved in sleep.

✠

Returning, just briefly, to Ireland. I have been to Portaferry, County Down, Ulster—the place of Father Vincent's birth and formative years—twice. The first time as a graduate student at London Business School on exchange from New York University. Those three months in London were, essentially, a holiday. I immediately met several fellow exchange students who have become lifelong friends. We were not always productive. To get out from the drink, and to explore a bit, I flew to Belfast. This was October 1994, a few years before the Good Friday agreement; perhaps I was overly sensitive, and being unable, as an outsider, to detect nuance, I could nevertheless sense a general tension in the city. For the first time in my life—and this is surely overly dramatic—I felt the burden of being hated for my faith. I was just a Yank, of course. And I was just a tourist, no doubt. But I was a believing Catholic. And my family was from Ulster. And I knew they had suffered for their faith.

Father Vincent never allowed a bitterness to seep into him regarding the Troubles. The situation is addressed in various writings by or about him, but one humorous comment he made later in his life about walking in those boots in Belfast bears mentioning:

> I remember once a few years ago walking in my habit in Belfast. (My early life had been spent in Belfast among Orangemen—you never knew what they would do.) I was wearing a very heavy pair of boots. I wondered if they threw me into the river would I sink, so I loosed my laces.[53]

But I was there to simply experience the city, and by foot. Father Vincent would have been proud of the number of steps I took over those few days, seeking context. Belfast is a lovely city, a decided mix of Irish and English influence in architecture and signage and personage, of course. I stayed in an apparently "mixed" area in a bed and breakfast. I walked and looked and studied and thought. I stopped into a pub in the middle of the day in a touristy area near majestic government buildings. I went out at night to a movie at a local university—St. Mary's, I think—and was amused by the keg of Guinness that was right there in the front row of the theatre; students would go and fill up and sit back down. Thinking it safer, I took a taxi ride down Shankill Road, the Protestant loyalist area with Ulster Freedom Fighter murals. I ate fast food. I prayed.

Two days in, I rented a car and drove for an hour to Portaferry, and was struck by its quietness and beauty, this little village at Strangford lough. It was a green, meandering drive. I can't fault myself for being an immature twenty-six, but I didn't do the things I would do now. I didn't go to St. Patrick's Church, where the family were parishioners, and where Ann McNabb had offered her son to St. Joseph at his baptism. I didn't visit the cemetery, where many family members are buried. I didn't attempt to visit my relative who was there living in the same McNabb family home.

My second visit to Portaferry was just four years later. I was living in Dublin when my brother Joe visited with a friend, and we took the drive up. I guess I can't fault myself for being stagnant in my faith, or having other priorities, but I didn't do those good things that time either. We did arrive on Fat Tuesday, though, and stayed above a pub. We made the most of it, of course. Staying overnight on Fat Tuesday meant we woke up there on Ash Wednesday, and that would have been a spiritually beautiful opportunity to get my ashes at St. Patrick's Church. I was too "out of sorts," after the previous night. For that matter, I didn't even think of it in that context. I remember just wanting to be back in Dublin, writing, and I idled the hours away that day walking about the small village center and down to the water.

One of the lasting memories I have was of the pub the next night. We were told by the locals the previous night that that was a raucous crowd, and to not expect the same the next day. It was true. The few young people we had met the night before met us back at the pub that night, but not to drink. They had all given up drink for Lent and, at least at that point, were sticking to it. It appears the North has held to the faith more than the South, actually. Perhaps that's because one is so identified by the Faith, by the opportunities, or, in the case of Catholics, traditionally, a lack of opportunities. I know it had affected the McNabb family in ways big and small.

Father Vincent's niece, Sr. Mary Magdalen, told the "famous" story of Father Vincent going on pilgrimage to Saul, not far from Portaferry, the landing-place of St. Patrick in Ireland. A monument is erected there, and a monastery. His motive was to pray for peace, as there had been three years of almost continuous religious persecution in Belfast and the surrounding area. True to form, she writes: "He dismissed the family at the church, left his big boots in the sacristy, walked through Portaferry barefoot, crossed the ferry, and then began his seven-mile tramp."[54] It is just anecdotal, she noted, but Sr. Mary said things did seem to settle down after that.

A more memorable anecdote of the family suffering for their faith is one that I have told my own children a number of times. From Father Vincent:

> When my father was a young shipmaster the Protestant ship-owner whom he served (and who shall be nameless) did not behave justly or honestly toward my father and his little family. From my mother's rare but painful references, I gathered that this ship-owner did not give us what my father had arranged to be given us of his earnings. As a result, my mother had hardly enough to keep her little ones for a very effective privation. She could never allow herself to speak of what this injustice of the ship-owner meant for us without indignation.
>
> One day when father was home between voyages we were told to prepare for a visitor. Our preparation consisted in being brought up to Sunday pitch of cleanliness and clothes. The boys of the family reported to each other the delivery of certain nice things to eat which we rarely saw on the family table. Altogether it was, perhaps, the most elaborate preparation for any guest we had ever seen. The secret was out when we were told not only to put on our best clothes but our best behaviour, because my father was going to entertain Mr. X—, his old ship owner!
>
> Something almost of histrionic drama, which many would interpret as melodrama, was in further fact that during the whole visit when a pauper was being given the alms of a feast, he was the ship-owner who emloyed my father; and my father (and a little less successfully) my mother served him as servants would serve their master.
>
> No doubt some of the good things to be eaten were given to us children; who thus shared at least in the leavings of the feast. But I now know three score years and ten that my father and mother had unconsciously given their children another and better feast which recalls Our Lord's words,

> "a fountain springing up into life everlasting." Perhaps on that day when they gave of their best to a Protestant who had wronged them most they gave to their wondering youngest son his first desire, never since quenched, of seeking to love even more than convert, "his separated brethren."[55]

The depth of this story is bottomless. The humility and example of James and Ann to their children. The restraint toward someone who wronged them, a man they relied on for their livelihood, which was considerable given all those children. It evokes, for me, the life of St. Joseph as revealed, mystically, to Sr. Maria Baij.[56] During the holy family's time in exile, Joseph had been shabbily treated by the local people seeking his carpentry services, who underpaid him, and some never paid him at all. Joseph's countenance, and his approach never changed. Jesus surely admired him for it.

I can only imagine that his father's even countenance influenced Father Vincent's perspective not just at the time, but in later years. It would have been so easy to give in to sectarian strife, as even many good religious people did, but Father Vincent never succumbed to that and was an impassioned champion of ecumenical relations and Christian unity. Among other notable efforts, he would even, as told later in this book, pray on his knees, in private, with the Archbishop of Canterbury, the head of the Anglican church, for just such an end.

WE CANNOT PROCEED much further without beginning to address the economic issues for which Father Vincent is perhaps best known. After the Bible and the *Summa,* no other writing influenced him so much as *Rerum Novarum,* the encyclical issued in 1891 by Pope Leo XIII, addressing the condition of the working classes.

It wasn't that Father Vincent was particularly politically or economically inclined. It was that he was particularly inclined toward *God.* And thus he was particularly inclined toward *souls.* His understanding of Truth was profound, through God's grace, and through God's gifts, which he worked tirelessly to develop. He understood we are embodied souls and the implications thereof. He knew our actions or inactions influenced the quality of our earthly life and determined our eternal disposition. He followed this to its logical end, acting as if one's eternal disposition, as evidenced by his deep concern for his own, should be the single greatest concern of one's life. It was certainly his mother's. She left New York for fear of losing her soul. She turned down the so-called American Dream. God called her back to Ireland. She listened. This certainly, as stated before, influenced him and the rest of the family. But one does not need human example, when concern for our eternal salvation is a basic tenet of our faith. All can, and should, arrive at this conclusion. All can, and should, make this their ultimate goal.

Father Vincent viewed our *being,* our way of life, in terms of the potential impact on our souls. Mr. Michael Hennessy, a former elected representative in the House of Commons, who has written extensively about Father Vincent and his contemporary, Hilaire Belloc, notes:

> Of course, the primary reason for Father McNabb's detestation of squalid and degrading urban conditions was the effect they had upon family life. The family is the prime unit of Christian society - indeed of any society - and precedes the State in every respect. Father McNabb knew that all economic, social, and political acts had some effect upon the family: it was by their effect upon the family that he would measure their worth or morality. The family was what he called "the Nazareth Measure."[57]

By Nazareth Measure, Father Vincent evoked the Holy Family. Siderman had this to say:

> Very often in his sermons and lectures he would extol what he called *small things*. "I do not like big things," he would say. "Look at Bethlehem. It was a small place. Our Lord was not born in a large house. Joseph and Mary did not live in such a place, their home was a small, intimate place," and then he pointed [across the street from Marble Arch] to the Cumberland Hotel, adding, "It was not like that. That is a White Elephant."

Father Vincent insisted on the importance of the family and said the world must look to the Holy Family at Bethlehem if it would return to sanity. He then continued: "Everything about the Holy Family was small, except their love of God, and in that they were great."[58] And Fr. Valentine offered his own summation of what Nazareth meant to Father Vincent: "deep down in his innermost soul he had the simplicity and utter consistency of a heart hidden in the Heart of Christ; his sole purpose was to glorify His Will. That is why Nazareth, Christ's way of life, *His* love of primary things became so precious to him and wedded him to the land."[59] Fr. Valentine's mention of "the land" and primary things, or *first things*, as Father Vincent so often referred to them, bear more mentioning. But first, this must be done in light of his relationship with two of the best-known men in England at the time, G. K. Chesterton and Hilaire Belloc.

✠

Of the many associations Father Vincent had in his lifetime, his relationships with the "twin towers" of English thought and letters in the early to mid-twentieth century, Hilaire Belloc and G. K. Chesterton, stood out. In these two men he found friendship alongside spiritual and intellectual companionship. Most notable was their common effort in the Catholic Land Movement, and in their endorsement and publicizing the economic theory Distributism.

Belloc was best known as a poet, historian, political activist and essayist and one of the few Catholic members of Parliament. Chesterton is legendary for his wit, his intellect, and his literary output. His way of turning a phrase (which Father Vincent mimicked at times; sometimes uncomfortably), earned him the nickname "The Prince of Paradox" for his ability to distill truths into small, often humorous bites that have endeared him to many to this day. The legacy of both men is still strong today, with various Societies in their names, and many of their books still in print. Chesterton, in particular, lives on with vigor. There are currently chapters of the Chesterton Society all over the world, and a network of Chesterton Academies (high schools) across the United States and in Italy, which take his personal charism as their charter. His Fr. Brown mysteries have proved enduring, having been adapted by the B.B.C. for television. The show is currently in its tenth season.

Bringing the three men together was idealism and seeking the betterment of themselves and society. In their attempts to address the challenges of post-Industrial Revolution life, before and between the World Wars, they found common cause. Just a few quotations about their feelings for Father Vincent before addressing their mutual efforts.

Belloc:

> The greatness of [Father Vincent's] character, his learning, his experience, and, above all, his judgment, was something

> altogether separate from the world about him. Those who knew him marveled increasingly at every aspect of that personality. But the most remarkable aspect of all was the character of holiness.[60]

Chesterton:

> I am nervous about writing what I really think of Father Vincent McNabb, but I will say briefly and firmly that he is one of the few great men I have met in my life; that he is in many ways—mentally and morally and mystically and practically—and that next to nobody nowadays has ever heard of him. But there is a further development which has already made a considerable difference, and that also is an interesting criticism of our time and of the type of effort needed to affect it, for at least nobody who ever met or saw or heard Father McNabb has ever forgotten him.[61]

And finally,

> at Father Vincent's Golden Jubilee celebrations at the London Priory. Father Vincent held forth for half an hour or more on the manner in which God had blessed his priestly life. Chesterton was sitting on one side of him and Belloc on the other. When Father Vincent had finished, Chesterton himself rose to say a few words of appreciation. I shall never forget his opening words.
>
> "When Father Vincent was speaking to us," he said very simply as he looked at him, "I felt as if I were in the presence of God."[62]

✠

Respect and mutual admiration aside, their common concern was for the welfare of society, which to them meant the welfare of souls. It was in their endorsement of Distributism and a simpler way of life on the land that their efforts were made practical. Though Father Vincent was a professed religious, they were all "men of the world." Father Vincent was not just a pious priest. He was one of eleven children and had watched his parents work hard to ensure the family's sustenance. His ministry exposed him to both the well-to-do and those on the margins. His own profound intellectual and spiritual gifts grounded him. In economic terms, he understood that the great sadness, pain and dysfunction of the world often resulted from a lack of understanding of "first things," things that are *necessary*. He would stress the difference between real and artificial needs; in other words, those things we authentically need to live—food, clothing, shelter, companionship—versus those that may contribute to a perceived elevated "quality of life."

In this, he recognized we do not live life purely on our knees in prayer. In fact, he would note: "Our first duty to God ... is not to pray, it is to work. Work is not our highest duty, but it is our first; God has made it so. All our life should be work or preparation for work, and our work should be for others." And Siderman remarked how in one such instance, he added for effect, and with humor, "it was quite possible Our Lady was scrubbing the floor at the moment of the Annunciation."[63]

So how does one do that? How does one live a life of work that is worthy of an offering to God, that is satisfying, that is not dehumanizing, that provides for one's needs? Though the nature of man's subsistence had been changing in various ways since the thirteenth century, the Industrial Revolution spurred a massive upheaval and eventually brought to the fore the downside to mechanized processes and the objectification of humans resulting from the lure of wage-labor.

It broke Father Vincent's heart to see the rural masses leaving the land to pack into flats to go off to factories for work, often in substandard conditions. We have already touched on the restrictions to personal and religious freedom that that led to (e.g., birth control, abortion, a living wage, etc.), not to mention the rote mechanization of the work itself.

There were very many critics at the time, and not a few movements which sought to remedy the "plight of the worker." Socialism and Communism, as yet untested, were gaining traction. A movement toward unionization was erupting in factories in Europe and North America. And, on a smaller scale, Father Vincent, Chesterton, Belloc and others were taking a deeper view of the *meaning* of work, the effects of the conditions in which it is done, and its impact on the soul.

Staying on the land, or returning to it, and a related economic system encouraging broad ownership of land and small business became a cause for which they advocated tirelessly. Dr. Tobias Lanz succinctly describes the overall effort in his Introduction to a 2003 reprint of the organizing document, *Flee to the Fields*, to which Father Vincent was a contributor. Lanz writes:

> *Flee to the Fields* was first published in 1934 as a collection of essays that articulated the basic ideas for the Catholic Land Movement. This movement had been formed in Glasgow, Scotland, in 1929 by clergy and laymen to re-establish an agrarian social economy that could counter the prevailing industrial regime. It was part of a broader social and intellectual movement known as Distributism, which advocated a widespread distribution of land and wealth among the general population. It was believed that a decentralized economy could better integrate economics with family and communal life and thereby create a more just and humane social order. The Catholic Land Movement was the most concrete and ambitious implementation of Distributist principles. It sought to demonstrate there was a workable alternative to Capitalism and Socialism, both of which were highly dependent on industrialization and massive urban populations for their survival.[64]

Father Vincent's primary concern, again, was the basic building block of society, the family. In fact, this was the very title of his essay contribution to the *Flee to the Fields*. In *The Family*, he highlights the family as a divine institution. Over the course of a concise ten pages, he highlights the inspired nature of the family, the proper relationship between the family and the State, the family and an economy, and the threats to the family as presented to it, particularly at that time.[65]

Over the course of several decades, the amount of ink spilled, debates engaged, sermons preached, meetings attended was considerable. Perhaps the singular achievement of their efforts was their involvement with a community of artists and craftsmen at Ditchling, in the English countryside, which was as close to a practical application of those concepts as they would get. Centered around the concepts of an intermingled work, faith and domestic life the inhabitants were involved in various occupations—sculptors, engravers, poets, writers, carpenters, weavers, leatherworkers, silversmiths and more—and included well-known men of the time: Eric Gill, Desmond Chute and Hilary Pepler, who founded the community. Many, under the encouragement of Father Vincent, became Dominican tertiaries. The community thrived for years, and Father Vincent spent considerable time there, learning to work the land (a minor part of the community) while providing spiritual guidance. Eventually, though, the community lost members through in-fighting and disillusionment and disinterest. It was also financially specious, and perhaps ironic, that capital was needed to expand. The death of Chesterton, Father Vincent's advancing years and Belloc's health problems served to lessen the winds of change. War, the Depression, and a society adapting to life in the current milieu rendered the concept quaint, and unrealistic, though many were sympathetic to the cause.

Fr. Valentine summarized the perspective and the disappointment of Father Vincent this way:

> That is why he condemned modern industrialism as an evil thing—its fruits were evil and could never be other than evil. Was he right in this judgment? And if his argument is false may there not still remain an element of prophecy in his preaching and propaganda? He believed with unshakable conviction that an "exodus" must come and that a second Moses would arise to lead God's people from the brickyards and organized slavery of the modern Egypt . . . [but even] if modern industrialism is inherently incompatible with God's order, as he thought, and of its very nature deleterious to the spiritual interests of mankind . . . the immediate propaganda of Vincent Joseph McNabb on which he set his heart failed lamentably.
>
> "As a priest," he had to confess, "I seem to realise when perhaps it is too late that Industrialism has won."[66]

✠

As a young man, James Joyce's description of hell in *The Portrait of an Artist as a Young Man* sent me into the confessional, where I sought not just absolution but advice, mostly related to the economics of my own life. In being later exposed to Father Vincent's and Chesterton's and Belloc's proposed remedies some few years later, I was enthralled. This made its way into my writing, and my short story about a failed back-to-the land experiment, "Herbert Wenkel Was Not Your Average Man," was published.

I struggled with balance when I was younger, attempting to reconcile how one makes money, how one sustains oneself and a family, while "seeking first the Kingdom of God." When shadow worlds are entered into, when man's penchant for "creativity" leads him toward different gods, toward materialism, toward self-centeredness, the economic environment we exist in will be perverted; this environment that is so elemental to the way we live. Father Vincent's point, at least partly, was the further "complicated" the environment, the less rooted we become, chasing after that which we cannot see—and, most importantly, by definition, that which can never satisfy. Virtue, and oftentimes even heroic virtue, is required to stay focused, to remain in His grace.

Ten years after that confession, immersed in my new career as a writer, and more aware of the ideal that Father Vincent and Hilaire Belloc and G. K. Chesterton and others espoused in terms of "going back to the land," but still immersed in a relatively mainstream family life, with my wife as breadwinner in corporate America, I wrote the following, which was ultimately published by the literary journal, *Rock & Sling*, and then became part of my first book, a short story collection entitled *The Body of This.* Here it is:

Herbert Wenkel Was Not Your Average Man[67]

> All right. Herbert Wenkel Was Not Your Average Man. Even though yes he did live in the middling suburbs of Boston in a neighborhood of gussied-up split-levels and capes. And even though yes he was a mid-level manager in Compliance at Berkley Financial downtown. And even

though yes, outwardly, things like his size and stature and looks and car and education were unremarkable.

But, it was Herbert's obsession with a New World Order that placed him at Feng's 8 Miles of Used Books just outside of Harvard Square every Saturday afternoon, standing in his Average Man uniform—boat shoes, Dockers, an old striped shirt—reading in the musty old stacks, dreaming of spades and hoes and seeds sinking into the lovely dark earth. Chesterton, Belloc. The Third Way. There, and not at home, so he could feel a little bit closer to them and to that, at least through the handiwork of the craftsmen from a different age, the soft cloth on all those fading spines, the smell of faded knowledge. He knew his thoughts were simple compared to theirs, but just like them he looked around and lamented ... *modernity* ... and he liked to say that he would have been better suited for medieval times—how much better would life be if you lived that much closer to death?—and it was no one thing in particular—just everything—on that particular Saturday when Herbert went home and convinced his wife Jilly that they should do in practice what those men could only write about.

She wasn't a pushover, but she was pliable, and she agreed, because to her, Herbert was quite extraordinary, and definitely not your average man; but also because standing all day long in retail was harder than it looked, and because her suburban idyll had long since faded gray, and because why the heck not when all she'd be leaving behind was what was right there, and so she said, "Yes, I'm ready for anything."

So Herbert and Jilly and their two young boys fled to northern Maine. They bought a small, crumbling dairy farm and apologized to the neighbors for being from Massachusetts and for knowing nothing—*absolutely nothing*—about dairy farming; and while they did know nothing about dairy farming if they could just figure out how to work within this here system they could make that type of living that they'd hoped to all along. But it took too long to see that there was a reason the people they'd bought from had sold. And while they couldn't afford to fix the broken down everything, Herbert pulled Jilly aside and said this wasn't how you were supposed to do it anyway. "Subsistence farming! Let's go off the grid!"

But Jilly just looked at him. *It gets worse than this?*

Herbert had always been decidedly mediocre when it came to reading his wife. He pressed on. "You remember what I told you? It's all about a different way, a third way, when you're beholden to none . . ."

Jilly was stone-faced. *Did he see what was here around him? This poverty of scratched-together existence?*

"What you do is, you sell as little as possible, you grow for yourself, and your whole life is a testament to . . ."

And then she was nearly frothed. *"No! We're too normal, too average, we can't go shitting in an outhouse and have our kids running around home-schooled. We can't do that. We couldn't even do this!"*

Herbert stepped back.

But Jilly wasn't done. "If you want to be closer to God do it on your own time! Do social work, downsize your priorities, but partake of the fruits of modernity. And let's get that 401(k) back to where it should be!"

On their ride back down the Maine Turnpike, Herbert tried to tell himself that while he had glimpsed a little bit of God in those northern Maine mornings—in the steaming potato fields, in the sun rising over the low-rolling mountains, in the feel of the hoe he'd clumsily scratched the ground with—back in that middling suburb he'd come from he'd also recognized God in places, just over a different, uglier landscape. At the same time, he knew he wanted something she didn't. Total devotion wasn't possible in that there first capitalistic system, at least not when you've got kids; if he was all alone he could have walked around ragged—or could he? Jilly would say that's not what He wanted, but Herbert wanted God to answer for him.

He waited. And in the meantime, they bought a gussied-up split-level, this time in a different middling suburb and just down the street from a whole new nation of colossal great-roomed dwellings that had seemed to just pop up overnight. Jilly went back to retail, and Herbert fell back into Compliance. And things were mostly back to normal. Except this time on Saturdays, instead of at Feng's 8 Miles of Used Books, you could find Herbert at home in his meager back yard, fumbling through his garden, squeezing dirt and waiting for a bit of that certain something he may never know.

Wenkel perhaps was your average man; a man who failed on the land. As I certainly would have. As most of us would. But to have told Father Vincent that at the time would have been a grave mistake. W. R. Titterton, Chesterton's first biographer, did, and barely lived to tell the following story:

> at one of the more private debates of the Distributist League, I myself felt the full force of the McNabb broadside. He had been telling all of us to flee to the fields. I got up and told him that I personally should do nothing of the sort. Citizens were needed as well as peasants and many of us (I certainly) would be useless on the land. When he replied, as he did at once, he fell upon me horse and foot. For some minutes (was that all it was?) I faced the thunderous charge of his eloquence. As I lay there, prostrate, but not unhappy, he turned to me and said: "I only say this because I love you." At the end of the meeting, he rushed at me, seized both of my hands and cried: "Oh my boy, forgive me." And much more. Did he set himself a penance for that? I shouldn't wonder.[68]

✠

In *Rerum Novarum*, Pope Leo makes the point that a free economic system is not sinful in itself; but that people who generate wealth have a responsibility to act morally, that "unrestricted capitalism" and the evils it can breed is at odds with God's wishes.

Personal wealth must be used for man's benefit. But just how much? This was the question that sent me to the confessional seeking the priest's absolution and advice. How much do I need to give to still maintain God's grace. Tithes? I still can't seem to get to that level. And then, whenever I hear of the widow offering her last two coins, I feel my shame.

Capitalism, for all the good it has done—and it is considerable—has enabled a shadow world that Father Vincent so often spoke of, and the "wealth" it has created has contributed, alongside other factors, to a departure from Truth. As humans need to hew to a morality, an ever-increasing level of corporate activism relating to moral issues has resulted.

Where this empowerment comes from—our descent into an individualist society that is actively anti-Christian—is a much more pressing issue than purely economic matters. So many of us no longer believe. Man is well on his way to supplanting Truth with a mock truth, a humanistic conception of truth molded after his own desires.

In economic terms, this has made its way into corporate America, into a "woke" capitalism, that has found its way into our products, our entertainment, and our way of life, and thus limits our very ability to make it through the day without engaging it to one degree or another, not to mention trying to avoid it in our work life. And so, quite simply, to Father Vincent's point, when we move beyond "primary things," the occasions for problems increase.

✠

I will get back to the business of Father Vincent's feet in a moment; it is necessary to wrap up this business of business, though, because of the reality of life in a fallen world, and the important role the topic played in Father Vincent's life and preaching. We need to subsist in this fallen world, and Father Vincent recognized this, of course. Remember that he stated our first duty in life is work (but that a higher duty is prayer). And so *how* we subsist is important, because *how* we work dictates so much. And this is why he was concerned with questions of economics and the means humans choose for sustaining ourselves. Those means impact that which is eternal—our souls—and *that* was truly his concern.

Father Vincent often remarked that another drawback to the prevailing economic environment was the emptiness of much of it. And this is due, in large part, to a lack of ownership. When you become a waged employee a mindset of *distance* settles in. When one is an owner there is a different sense of responsibility and, quite often, a different level of interest and engagement. We can see, in a particular way, the desolation of a good portion of wage work.

The Covid pandemic prompted an unforeseen response to

a fundamental truth that has been latent in the workforce for decades: that being a simple cog lacks fulfillment. Those on the lowest rungs, hourly workers in service jobs or retail, recognized that there is more to work than what they were receiving, both remuneratively and in terms of satisfaction. The question, "Why am I doing this?" has come to the fore, and despite the dark undertones of a "Great Reset," it is understandable. Many of those jobs remain unfilled.

Belloc described a related dynamic in his book, *The Servile State*. In simplistic terms, the book decries the inevitable convergence of big business and the state. Belloc argues pure capitalism is not really practicable, and laws and protections will inevitably pop up, ensuring the perpetuation of a system in which there are owners and many more workers who rely on those owners. Perhaps the best-known quote from the book is "the control of the production of wealth is the control of human life itself." Indeed. But how we address this is much more textured.

Part of the problem, Father Vincent would say, is size. Small is, in so many ways, more *human*. The concept of subsidiarity—that which can be controlled by the closest entity to the source, should control it—looms large. The Distributist movement encouraged broad ownership.

Quite simply, my own struggles with the issue of how we are to subsist are a post-modern problem. I grew up in a family of modest means, in a time of great excess, in a society in which one can better one's financial standing. When I was younger, I struggled with my desire to accumulate wealth, to address whatever I perceived to have been lacking in my childhood, but more specifically, to keep pace with those around me. And as I got older, I struggled with the means by which we accumulate wealth, recognizing the greed that is almost inherent in the system, but also the emptiness of the pursuit. Father Vincent's prescription was never far from my awareness. His books *Nazareth or Social Chaos* and *The Church and the Land* and other seminal documents of the Catholic Land Movement, along with Distributist literature and the influential book,

Small is Beautiful (a title Father Vincent would have loved), offered a comforting alternative. But I always felt these options were unrealistic.

In the midst of my struggle, I came across a book, *The Church and the Market: A Catholic Defense of the Free Economy*, written by Thomas E. Woods, Jr. In this, too, there was a Father Vincent connection. Mr. Woods is a devout Catholic, and a Harvard educated economist and Fellow at the Mises Institute, an organization that embraces the so-called Austrian School of Economics, which proposes as little government involvement in regulation of the economy as possible. Seeking to reconcile economic things, to understand what it is that we are called to do to sustain ourselves in this life, feeling apathetic about my MBA from a top business school, and frustrated and guilty that I could not practically embrace any type of Back to the Land lifestyle, or envision any form of widespread employment of the economic principles behind Distributism, I read the book eagerly to affirm, hopefully, my struggle to reconcile modern life with Catholic spirituality. Mr. Woods' words were hopeful to me. He writes:

> Partisans of the market are often portrayed as morally stunted for their emphasis on economic efficiency, an emphasis that supposedly fails to reckon with other values whose importance is said to be greater than that of mere efficiency. But the point is, the more efficient we are in producing the goods we need, the more leisure we can enjoy to pursue the very "higher things" that economists allegedly leave out of account. The more capital-intensive our economy the greater the productivity of labor, the greater the output, the greater our overall wealth, and the less time we need to work in order to earn the money to purchase the goods we need . . . greater leisure and greater wealth are precisely what make it possible for people to spend more time doing the things in life that really matter.[69]

This was hopeful to me; though I can't, now, get out of my head Father Vincent's speaking in detail about how the words "efficiency" and "progress" were often used for evil's end.[70] And as for the issue of more leisure, Father Vincent saw excessive leisure as troubling. With four teenagers, I can attest to this. Siderman recounts,

> I once heard Fr. McNabb surprise and antagonize some of his audience by saying that there was danger in people having too much leisure time. In reply to a chorus of dissenting voices he gave it as his opinion that most people do not know how to use leisure in a proper manner. That going to the cinema several times a week, or going to dog or horse racing, were not the best ways of spending leisure hours, although going occasionally might not do great harm. "Idle hands and idle minds," he said, "Frequently lead to occasions of sin. People do not know how to use their minds apart from the ordinary things. How many can sit quietly and contemplate the deep things of life? They must have noise like the blare of the radio. "Leisure," he stated, "was the only preparation for doing useful work, but in this modern world much of the work done was useless and often harmful."[71]

Finally, to my surprise, Mr. Woods addressed in detail, and quite deftly, the concept of Distributism, ultimately arguing against its practicality. This paragraph sums up my thoughts at the time (and directly inspired my story, "Herbert Wenkel Was Not Your Average Man"):

> Practically anyone in the United States today who possess the requisite knowledge and modest capital can acquire farmland and chase after the kind of self-sufficiency advocated by Belloc. Producing their own necessities and in possession of the means of production, so to speak, such a family would be utterly independent of employers or anyone else. They would also enjoy a standard of living so depressed and intolerable as to throw the rationality of the entire enterprise into question. This certain outcome probably accounts for why the overwhelming majority of people choose to take their chances within the division of labor, balancing the risks from which this earthly life is never entirely secure against the unparalleled wealth and comfort they can enjoy by not retreating into semi-autarky.[72]

I reached out to Mr. Woods, telling him of my relation to

Father Vincent, whom he, of course, was very familiar with. Operating as Mr. Woods did in the world of economic theory, and also being a devout Catholic, he had butted heads with modern Distributists. I told him I had a hard time envisioning a practical employment of Distributism and agreed with much of what he wrote. Mr. Woods was gracious in his response, but perhaps also saw his opportunity. Here was a relative of Father Vincent McNabb, one of the best known Distributists—a father of Distributism, even—and even *he* sees Distributism as impractical. He asked if he could quote some portion of my email to him on a widely read blog and I agreed. Though I didn't say anything I didn't believe to be true, the way in which my comment was framed by Mr. Woods was opportunistic.

When I saw his posting of my comments, I felt sick. I recognized I had, to some extent, betrayed my beloved uncle.

FOR REFRESHMENT, let's return, for a bit, to Father Vincent's younger years, where pious activities can be seen from the time he was child. His erecting an altar in his bedroom has already been mentioned, but he was also drawn to the particular opportunity to visit with God in consecrated places. My great-grandfather, Patrick, recounts the following story:

> Canon Dunne, the saintly Pastor of our Parish Church, St. Michael's in Elswick, having seen Joe praying in his Parish Church, said one day to my mother, "Mrs. McNabb, you have a wonderful boy in Joseph, an extraordinary boy. If I stepped into our church for a visit, it is more likely that I would find him there on his knees. If I am passing the Cathedral and go in for a short visit, it is equally possible that I would find him there ahead of me. One day, when I was passing St. Andrew's Church, which, as you know, is quite a distance away from my own church, I went in for a brief visit and there, sure enough, was Joseph on his knees, lost in deep meditation.

This is not surprising to me at all. He was holy from an early age. He had a depth of *awareness* and the gift of deep faith, which he cultivated. He was called. He answered. I can envision a young Joe McNabb being called to His presence in the tabernacle, leaving his older brothers in their games, as my great-grandfather, recounted, at the hearing of a church bell ringing. I can sense his restlessness, his desire to move. I can understand his setting out on foot, to think, and to head in the direction—knowingly, or unknowingly—of a church. Is there a more beautiful and comforting feeling walking into a Catholic church in a distant city or merely a few towns away? Some of my favorite memories are being with my wife and children at Mass in such varied places as Quebec City, Greensboro (North Carolina), Montreal, New Bedford, Boston, Westford (Massachusetts), Newport (Rhode Island), Philadelphia, Hampton (Virginia), Hampton (New Hampshire), Lewiston and Kennebunk, and many more. To sit with God in a new setting, amongst unknown fellow worshipers, delighting in their own devotion in being there, freshens the experience, and has great spiritual benefit.

Most of all, it is comfort. Sitting in the presence of the Almighty. For a restless and desirous soul, like Father Vincent's, and my own, it is comfort. That God is there, so present, is comfort, and knowledge that everything will be all right.

✠

Why have we gone to Mass in so many different cities? One word, primarily: basketball. My boys have grown up playing club (AAU) basketball and while that has been a blessing, it has also been a challenge. It is yet another sign of the times that Sundays are seen as no different than any other day, another battle in this world, this battle against the loss of faith, the lack of reverence and acknowledgment of the sacred. Weekend basketball has provided opportunity to witness, of course. To find local churches, to drag an exhausted kid away from the team, leaving the alt-cathedral of a gym on the Lord's Day to find a true one.

I am reminded of the lines that form on Sundays outside the brunch spots here in my "foodie" city, and of a column in the *New York Times* that would run on Sundays. A famous New Yorker would be asked what their Sundays consisted of. Usually the answer involved brunch, walks in Central Park and the like. New York is both a great and terrible place, and those things mentioned above are good, but over the course of the years of reading that column I don't recall any of those interviewed mentioning going to a religious service. I do remember mention, more than a few times, yoga.

✠

When he was a boy, Joe, the youngest of the McNabb boys, was always trying to keep up with his very physical older brothers. He was frailer than they, and seemingly less capable. Fr. Valentine has a great deal to say about this in terms of his subject's developing psychology. I am no expert on biographies, but Fr. Valentine seems to have overreached in his ascribing certain psychological tendencies to Father Vincent based on this. I do recognize, though, the impact of one's early experiences, and this has made me consider, here as I get older, not just my own life's influences, but those of my children. And so I say, basketball is good. But it is also potentially bad.

The game was introduced to England early after its invention, which would have been when Father Vincent was just a young man, though I am guessing he never heard of it. While many people know the creator of the game was James Naismith, most do not know this Canadian son of Scottish immigrants was a Presbyterian minister. Naismith's intent with sport was to bring souls to Christ, and of that Father Vincent would have greatly approved.

I have encouraged my boys to play basketball, and they have and they do. As they have gone along, I have encouraged them to approach the game with eyes on God, and with spiritual benefit in mind. It's not easy. Early on in my own spiritual journey, the words of St. Francis de Sales in *Introduction to the Devout Life*, regarding competition,[73] struck home. Writing mostly of games of chance, which he instructs to avoid, but also healthy pastimes, he recognizes the occasions for sin. This may seem severe, but whenever the ego is provoked, there is danger.

In this day of social media highlight videos and the homage paid to sports superstars, the soul is ripe for, if not sin, then at least discouragement. C. S. Lewis's Screwtape was correct in his instructing his demon nephew, "To be, is to be in competition." It is true, mostly; because we let it be. I endorse the competition, the "muscular Christianity" that Naismith sought to inspire, but I recognize the pitfalls.

St. Sebastian, patron saint of athletes, and Blessed Pier Giorgio Frassati, lay Dominican and athlete, pray for us!

✠

Those early displays of piety and longing to be in Christ's presence in Church, led, unsurprisingly, to an inclination toward the priesthood. Young Joseph McNabb initially expressed interest in the secular priesthood (becoming a parish priest), but was ultimately drawn to the Dominicans, though he felt unworthy. His oldest sister, Mary, whose daughter, Annie, so influenced by Father Vincent, became a Dominican nun (Sr. Mary Magdalene), introduced him to the Dominicans at Woodchester and encouraged him. Sr. Mary Magdalene writes:

> It was my mother, Father Vincent's eldest sister, Mary, who first introduced him to the Dominicans. My grandfather had talked things over with him, with a view to settling his career in life. Joe had just come home to Newcastle upon Tyne from St. Malachy's college, Belfast. Grandfather [Father Vincent's father, James] suggested various professions, for he was anxious to give Joe every chance as he was the youngest boy of the family and very intelligent, but Joe turned down every proposal. At last, my grandfather became exasperated. "Look here, boy," he said, "is there anything you would like?" Said Joseph, "Yes, a tin of condensed milk": for he loved condensed milk.
>
> Grandfather of course was very annoyed at this, but some days later my mother [Father Vincent's sister, Mary,] who had heard about all this scene, took Joe with her when she went to visit her confessor, Fr. Louis Weldon, O.P. at St. Dominic's Priory. As soon as they got into the guest room, Joe said: "This is where I want to be. I want to be a Dominican."[74]

The anecdote is noteworthy on many levels, not the least of which is the cheekiness of young Joe's response. I can see that type of response from one of my own teenagers. Father Vincent is so emblazoned as Friar, that seeing this adolescent reaction is refreshing and humanizing. His response also speaks to the fact that James McNabb's children were afraid of him. It was mentioned previously that he ran the household not unlike he ran his ships. The boys, in particular, were not displeased when he was away from home for long journeys. Captain James McNabb, himself, remarked later in life of his strong regret regarding how he had handled the boys. There had been a distance between them, which closed measurably in the last years of his life, as this capable seaman grew frail and ill.

Though Mary knew of her brother's desire, their parents did not. Eventually, it was agreed that he would become a parish priest in Belfast. But when, upon the arrangement of Mary, two friars showed up one day to speak to their parents, there was confusion and consternation. My great-grandfather tells the story:

> when two Dominican fathers called at our house one day and said they would like to see my father and mother, there was much speculation as to the purpose of their visit, except, of course, in the minds of Joe and my sister, Mary. It so happened that my father was home at the time, and I remember that he and my mother received the visiting fathers in the front room, where they conferred together behind closed doors. After a short time, Joe was called in. Then it was that we began to wonder whether he was thinking of becoming a Dominican. After a lengthy conference with my parents, the priests left. When they had gone, I was sitting alone in the back parlour, which, in a sense could be called my father's den … my father soon entered the room, filled his pipe with tobacco, lit it and sank into his armchair with a very worried look on his face. Not a word was spoken until my mother entered the room a few minutes later. My father was the first to break the silence. He said to my mother: "Well, what do you think of it Ann? Don't you think it's terrible?" My mother replied: "Well, James, I would not look at it that way. I really think Joe knows what he is doing. You heard him say that he had given this matter serious consideration. He has consulted his Father Confessor on the subject and is finally convinced that God is calling him to the Dominican Order. You also heard what he said about the seriousness of interfering with God's Will in this affair. So we must not act hastily." We, too, must give the matter our most serious consideration, before we come to a final decision.

> According to my mother, what upset her father more than anything else was when the vow of poverty was being explained to them by the two fathers and when they were told that, according to the terms of the vow, a Dominican cannot claim any possessions as his own, not even the clothes on his back. It was then that my father flew off the handle and told them bluntly: "I'll never, no I'll never consent to a child of mine becoming a voluntary pauper!" Anyway, my parents finally gave their consent to Joe's entry into the Dominican Order; and that father, who had raised such a fuss over the vow of poverty, himself became a Tertiary of St. Dominic. When he was laid to rest, after his long and hazardous seafaring life, he had the great grace of being clothed and buried in a habit[75] which had belonged to his Dominican son.[76]

This is a beautiful story of, despite doubt, relenting to God's will and the great fruit that will inevitably bear. That James McNabb was laid to rest in one of Father Vincent's habits is so poignant—and he was not the only McNabb with a Dominican vocation to be laid to rest in such. My great-grandfather was, too.

✠

Throughout his ministry as a Dominican, Father Vincent was busy working for souls—you might say *walking* for souls—hurrying from one place to the next throughout each day to but he couldn't not notice his surroundings. He was too in love with God not to witness His creation, and, particularly in London, the most glorious of his creation—souls. These two little accounts of his tell as much:

> I was walking in a squalid part of East London the other day when I saw a small child seated on a doorstep nursing another little one smaller than herself. It was quite evident from the state of their cheeks they were eating sweets of some rather adhesive substance. The smaller child, wrapped in a rather grubby shawl, was somewhat frightened of me, but the other one nursing the small beshawled object seemed to think it quite all right. She smiled shyly and said, "Hallo, guv'nor" and offered me a sweet from a penny poke bag. I had a new inspiration

> about Our Blessed Lady as if she might offer me a sweet if she saw me.[77]

How a simple scene on a simple walk can evoke visions of Mary. And now, below, how common interactions can raise the eyes and heart to God.

> A little group of Protestant children near the priory seem to have taken into their heads that I am a fairly friendly object. They wave to me across the street. It always brings tears to my eyes. I say, "God be merciful to me, a sinner." I've never given them anything except a smile. One tiny little thing ran with arms outstretched as if I were Mother coming home with lovely things from the market.[78]

Father Vincent took to heart Jesus' words, "unless you turn and become like children, you will not enter the kingdom of heaven" (Matthew 18:3). He had great respect for children, for their as-yet unjaded insight and innocence. The following from Siderman summarizes this perfectly:

> Although Fr. McNabb told us he was not sentimental, nevertheless he could be deeply moved by "little things", and by little children. A Dominican Sister teacher had sent him an essay on the Crucifix, written by a little girl aged six, and this so impressed and moved him, that he wrote a booklet entitled, *Of Such is the Kingdom*, in which he expressed wonder and joy that one so young could have written so finely; for, though it contained less than seventy words, it was worthy to be compared with what had been written by the greatest writers. He confessed that reading the child's words had brought a sob into his heart.[79]

One might think that preaching at the level and frequency he did, Father Vincent would be dour or pessimistic or in a perpetual state of finger wagging, but, again, he was known for his love and his great joy. True joy resides in holiness. In holiness is understood the *source* of joy, of happiness, of fulfillment—of freedom. True joy resides in understanding what it means to be human; that we are created in His image, and that we are, should we choose to be, saved. For eternity. Father Vincent so very much wanted this joy for others, recognizing not just the horror of that other eternal fate, but also the fulfilment in the present. For him, joy was right reason. Joy was family. Joy was simple things, small things. Joy was God. And he knew God. Intimately.

As Fr. Valentine recounts,

> A Father once told us that when passing by Father Vincent's room shortly after he had settled down to sleep, a tired voice murmured, "And now, dear Lord, please go away, Brother Vincent wants to sleep."[80]

This account is so very telling; that there is a conversation here. And in any meaningful conversation there are *two* voices. In most prayer lives, there is usually just one—ours, and, if we are honest, that voice is occasionally giving thanks but more often than not, asking for something.

In this account—this most beautiful account—it appears Jesus is quite talkative (perhaps because we rarely give him the opportunity to speak!). And it must be something joyfully routine He is saying, because Father Vincent clearly wouldn't beg off from the conversation otherwise. And given Father Vincent's response, their being in conversation is not an unusual occurrence.

Siderman backs this up, observing,

> It was noticeable, sometimes, that when he was speaking on a deeply religious or holy subject, he would appear to forget his audience for a moment, gaze at and touch the large wooden crucifix that was always over the platform, or peer into the distance to Tyburn Road, as though seeing Tyburn. Then he would remember us, smile, and continue his remarks.[81]

His being entranced and likely hearing God's voice, is *relationship,* and evidence of a man who followed the counsel of St. Paul, who said, "Rejoice always. Pray constantly" (1 Thessalonians 5:16–18). Joy was being with Christ. Joy was having a relationship with him. With the personage of Christ. It is available to all of us, at all times. We are better if we have that. Father Vincent knew this. He lived in Christ's presence. His whole life was testimony to this. From his habit as a sign of devotion (and on those London streets, a "sign of contradiction"), to his boots, worn from his using his God-given feet, to his bare cell free from distraction, to his tirelessly ministering to souls to the point of exhaustion every day.

It can be hard being joyful in these times, when the griping is incessant, when we are bombarded with the thoughts and arguments and vainglory and stupidity of the world, when we are so polarized, even within the Church—bishops against bishops, cardinals against cardinals. But we are to maintain equanimity. We are to give to Jesus our frustrations and sufferings. We are to talk to Him, as Father Vincent did, and listen for His voice. We are to live simply, and focus on His great love for us. In this, there is joy. And we would do well to reflect on that beautiful scene, of Father Vincent having said good night to a talkative, playful Jesus, his dropping down to that wood floor that was his bed, polished so handsomely, for so many years, by his hands, still in his Dominican habit, his outstretched arm his pillow, for a night of restful sleep, secure in his Lord.

✠

More about sleep (of all things) in a moment. Now, about those hands that polished. Siderman writes:

> Apart from the well-worn black and white habit, the famous old boots and the thick white knitted socks, there was something else about him which must have seemed strange to many who did not know him well; and that strange something was his hands. Most people would expect the hands of a priest to be soft and white, well cared for, like the hands of a person who did not do manual labour. Not so the hands of Father McNabb. His hands were gnarled and large, often reddened, and appearing to be swollen, the hands of a labourer. And so, it was, for though a priest, he also laboured. It is a fact that he regularly scrubbed the floor of his room, and kept it clean, and also washed some of his garments. A friend has told

> me that going into his Church one day, he found Father McNabb with a mop washing the chapel floor. His feet and ankles bare, his habit drawn up, the hood over his head, while washing he was always praying and, having at last finished his task, he passed by the High Altar, genuflected deeply, and went on his way.[82]

✠

Now sleep. An interesting point Fr. Valentine makes is with regard to sleep. Father Vincent was so engrossed in his goal of winning souls for Christ, he worked to the point of daily exhaustion. It was certainly not easy, dealing with the trauma of the world, as confessor, and debater, and sentient soul who surely recognized the darkness. He lived amidst the battle, but "Not even [that] deprived him of a single night's sleep."[83] That speaks to a soul, ultimately, at peace. It is easy to rest well if you put in a good days work, trust in Him and recognize that despite whatever challenges and setbacks you encounter, you will achieve that most meaningful accomplishment: heaven. Regarding sleep, Fr. Valentine told this story:

> I remember Father Vincent telling me how tragic it was that so many of our young Fathers were falling ill through overwork. "And the odd thing is," he said, "that so many people think I am eccentric. It is very fashionable these days to burn the midnight oil, all *ad majorem Dei gloriam* no doubt; but I'm eccentric because after a full day's work I retire every night promptly at ten. Then again I'm eccentric because I wear so few clothes and yet isn't it the other folk with their winter woolies and mufflers who are always catching cold? I haven't had a cold for years; and it is thirty years since I had 'flu, and I only took it then because I very foolishly overworked when giving a retreat at St. Dominic's."[84]

And in a letter to his niece, Sr. Mary Magdalen, O.P.:

> My dearest niece,
>
> I feel just a little alarmed about those neuralgia head-pains which you say you now suffer ... You also say you are often tempted to stay up at night. I implore of you not to think of staying up at night in order to shorten

> the time of sleep. Nothing should be shortened so little as sleep … Don't let anything eat into your sleep. Nature will demand its due, and demand interest as well … your seeming selfishness in this matter of sleep is really love of your sisters.[85]

In his falling quickly asleep each night, Psalm 4:8–9 is evoked:

> But you have given my heart more joy
> than they have when grain and wine abound.
> In peace I will lie down and fall asleep,
> for you alone, LORD, make me secure.

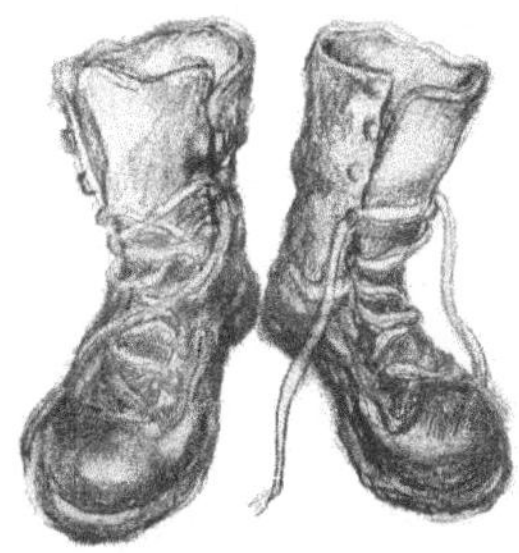

THERE ARE MANY REFERENCES to Father Vincent's cell at St. Dominic's. Perhaps the most touching comes from E. A. Siderman, who, given their relationship, was granted access to the cell after Father Vincent's passing. He writes:

> By the great kindness of Father Prior of St. Dominic's Priory, I have been privileged to visit the cell that was the home, for many years, of Fr. McNabb. It is on an upper floor, a small room, containing the barest necessities, a bed, a small table, a chair. Yet he even denied himself the comfort of the bed and the chair. The kind friar, who accompanied me to the room and who had been so close to Fr. McNabb for so many years, told me quite simply that Fr. McNabb never slept on his bed. He slept on the bare floor, alongside the bed, the bare floor that he had himself scrubbed so often, and on which he lay with just a blanket for covering. Neither did he ever sit on his chair—he either stood or knelt—and when reading or writing, he placed his book or writing paper on the small table and knelt against it. Also in the room there was an old style high-back armchair which, I was told, was put into the room and in which after much persuasion he rested during his last hours, while his life was drawing to a close. Standing in this room and hearing these words, I felt humbled and yet strangely exalted, and on leaving it, I felt I had left a room that had become hallowed.[86]

There is a lot here. The most significant is Siderman feeling the aura of sanctity present in the cell. This was a hard-won aura, the end result of a life of devotion. But it goes even deeper than this. No life is lived in sum, but in the compiling moments and minutes and hours and days and years. If we analyze that cell and its former inhabitant's ways, let us remember the many detractors Father Vincent suffered, particularly those who dismissed his eccentricities as vanity. Equally, let us remember the many who were amused by the accounts of Father Vincent doing some such eccentric thing, who, when attempting to sum up the man, would mention things like his boots or his worn habit or his sleeping on the floor of his cell. It is easy to dismiss someone based on an outward action. It is easy, too, to define someone by mention of their habits, or to be amused by them and then move on. But let us consider more deeply that a charlatan cannot last, and that actions of momentary fervor are just that. Neither would characterize Father Vincent.

Father Vincent's eccentricity was really, in most cases, holy asceticism. It was intentional and it was an offering and was neither vainglorious in seeking approval from man nor momentary in religious fervor. Spend one night on the floor when an empty bed is next to you. The allure of that soft comfort would draw the charlatan in. The soul experiencing the glow of fervor could perhaps persist for a time, but that is not the way of God. We must all suffer dryness and doubt, and thus that bed would cry out, and a less devoted soul would eventually heed it.

Father Vincent sleeping on the floor of his cell is not a "nice" or "interesting" story. It is the story of a soul whose every fiber yearned for God. Night after night he would be reminded, perhaps every time he rolled over on that hard floor, that his life was not his own. The deep callouses that were purported to be on his hips were evidence of authentic love, intentional giving, and physical devotion. As Dominicans, we are encouraged to pray with our bodies, and this was just one more way to do it.

✠

And regarding Dominicans praying with our bodies, St. Dominic composed nine ways of prayer, recognizing the body as an opportunity for reverence. These nine ways of prayer are: deep bowing, lying face down, self-flagellation, repeated genuflection, standing ramrod straight before a crucifix with hands in the manner of a book, standing with arms outstretched, stretching to heaven hands above head, sitting quietly recollected, and finally, the ninth way, and so fitting in the context of this discussion: *walking.*

✠

It was described that the floor of his cell was gleaming. That Father Vincent would be on his knees moving about the room sweeping it with his hands. That floor was symbolic of so much, perhaps mostly of its cleanliness and his sweeping, as if sweeping the sin from his soul. On that floor, standing, or more often, on his knees, he wrote. Copiously. Books and sermons and retreat notes and letters and poetry and more. Is there a more beautiful or obvious intent? The very act states, *I am on my knees. This, what I am doing, is an offering.*

It is not lost on me that while my intentions may be the same, and while I begin my writing day, as I always do, on my knees, I am writing this while sitting in a chair.

✠

Might there have been some measure of pride that Father Vincent took in his boots? Yes. Sinful pride? I don't think so. As we saw in his elaborate request for his own funeral as a means to preach even in death, his boots served a purpose. But did he preach with them? Yes. As Fr. Mark Heath, O.P., remarked, his boots, "were a sermon to all on his social doctrine of the crafts,"[87] as his boots had been made by a craftsman at Ditchling. And his habit, too. That his boots were worn down was testimony to the world regarding the virtues of frugality and industry. Father Vincent was always quick to point out where his boots and habit came from. It was, as he saw it, "good advertising," and evidence of life well-walked.

✠

For a number of years, I had my own pair of thick, black boots. Doc Martins. I loved those boots. I even walked quite a bit in them, so much so that I wore down a particular spot on both heels. I was amused by that, not because of any likeness to Father Vincent wearing down his own boots, but just because it spoke to a certain way I walked, my gait, and it was unexpected. I also, if I am being honest, liked the way the boots looked. No shame in that, I suppose. This came early in my writing career. And like the scraggly beard I grew when I moved to Ireland, these boots, too, were an outward sign of who I was trying to become. I guess I was self-conscious (Lord, forgive my ego and pride). Our clothes do represent us, make a statement, as intentional or as unintentional as that may be. When I worked in finance in Manhattan, I wore high-end suits and cuff links. That was a projection. A projection I was never comfortable with. My shoes at the time, they were symbolic, too.

There is one particular walk in those shoes I remember above all, because I never wanted it to end. It was in Washington, D.C. I was post-M.B.A., but pre-writing. I was there for business. I didn't want to be. I was wearing my Cap Toe Oxfords. I still have them (twenty-five years later) and they are my one and only real pair of shoes. Nice shoes, *Barney's New York* (R.I.P.). But they were like leaded weights. Not just metaphorically, but physically. So heavy, heavy. So clunky with a big heel. And so bad for my surgically reconstructed left knee. I didn't like walking in them, but I remember floating in them that afternoon. I was in between meetings, and I was alone and I could think about whatever I wanted to. I remember the relief, and the possibility. I remember looking at my watch and timing how long I could go before I had to turn back, and being so *preciously relieved* on my way out, and so *wanting time to crawl* on my way back. I would be returning to some such meeting or other, when what I *really* wanted to do was walk.

It wasn't long before I made that happen, chucking it all and moving to Ireland. And then I got those boots. I even wore them with shorts. And then I had kids. And then my back went out, and I needed something lighter and more supportive. And now I wear, mostly, running sneakers. Perhaps that is symbolic of something, too.

✠

Years ago, I was inspired by the boots of another Vincent. When I bought a print of van Gogh's *A Pair of Shoes,* I imagined the boots in the painting were what Father Vincent's would have looked like. I have since seen the full-length portrait of a standing Father Vincent (he refused to sit down), painted by the portraitist Sir James Gunn, and there is a glimpse of those boots, looking, indeed, van Gogh-esque. Van Gogh's "shoes", both left, side-by-side, have been the subject of much speculation by art historians and regular folks alike, but what cannot be debated is the feeling of them, and the spirituality thus derived. Philosophers and critics Martin Heidegger, Meyer Schapiro, and Jacques Derrida have all spent time dissecting the spiritual meaning of van Gogh's boots.[88] To me, they are worn evidence of a simple life of dignified struggle. That they are both left feet signifies two people beautifully shared that journey.

FR. VALENTINE was explicit in describing his book, *Father Vincent McNabb, O.P., A Portrait of a Great Dominican,* as not a biography. He writes:

> I ask the reader to keep this in mind. What follows is not an official biography; it is not, strictly speaking, a biography at all, but merely an attempt on the part of one of Father Vincent's students and brethren to explain him—to make sense of what for many, even of his most ardent admirers, still remains *inexplicable.*[89]

What was *inexplicable* was that Father Vincent was *unusual.* He was unusual in his ways, and in his dress. He was unusual in his intellect, and in his holiness. He was unusual in his manner, and in his methods. He was unusual in that he elicited strong reactions, both positive and negative, not just from the general public, but even amongst his brethren. Fr. Valentine writes:

> To some he was superficial, a mountebank, a lover of the limelight. "To me," wrote one old Dominican Father, "he was not a saint, but a poseur; and a saint's evidence of holiness [were really] just a mass of eccentricities. The Apostle was lost in the comedian all too often."
>
> At the other extreme were those for whom Father Vincent was one of the few great men of the century, a portent, a prophet, holy, utterly sincere and beyond all criticism.[90]

There is no shortage of examples of holy men and women in the Church being castigated by society, and even—and perhaps even especially—by members of their own religious orders. It would not be appropriate to compare Father Vincent to great and notable saints throughout the ages who suffered at the hands of their communities, but who were ultimately vindicated. First, he was not limited in his ministry as many of those great saints were. He had his detractors, to be sure, but they fell along the lines of cultural traditionalists not in the religious sense, but in a societal sense. Father Vincent, to their taste, may have lacked a certain decorum. He behaved differently than what was expected. It should be remembered that, though Irish, his ministry took place, by and large, in that land of customs, traditions and etiquette—England. Outside the faith, his detractors were those he jousted with.

And, in a surprising next statement, at least for those who have only heard of the man superficially, Fr. Valentine continues: "I can only hope that the knowledge of this great priest's personal struggle will help us all to face our own spiritual trials with courage."[91] And what was that struggle? Fr. Valentine does not, succinctly, tell us. It is not quite scrupulosity, and certainly not vice or impurity or disbelief. I believe that great struggle was not a struggle at all, but a restlessness, a vigorous and relentless activity residing in his overwhelming desire for God, for heaven, for peace.

✠

One way he addressed that restlessness was work. *Rerum Novarum* was "sacred" to Father Vincent, as Fr. Valentine points out.[92] That would be primarily due to its central point, addressing the condition of the working classes. Indeed, that document and its prescription inspired, after the Gospel itself, his efforts to steering men and women back to the land, and toward smaller, more meaningful means for sustaining oneself in this world. However, another point was no less influential. In the document, Pope Leo XIII instructs, "Every minister of holy religion [to] bring to the struggle the full energy of his mind and all his powers of endurance."[93]

Father Vincent's level of activity was legendary. He was described by his brethren as having boundless energy. He was tireless in pursuit of souls. He understood what was at stake. He was given his vocation by the Lord. He did all he could to honor that, and was motivated in no small part by his yearning, by his desire for peace. I do believe this was not anxiety, per se, but was a natural outlet for his great desire for the Lord. And his daily regimen is partly, no doubt, a reason for the consistency and quality of his aforementioned sleep.

A glimpse of his industriousness is evident in letters to his brother Laurence, over the course of several months. He writes:

> So many things are calling upon me that I must leave some of them over. Tonight, I shall address a Meeting at Nottingham; and on Thursday night I am one of the guests at the Leicester Parliamentary Debating Society.
>
> This Easter season has been unusually busy. Imagine me giving a course of six lectures on Political Economy! My excuse is that I know nothing about the subject. But I am anxious to give some of our coming public men and women an interest in what must always be the foundation of the best public work.
>
> Life at Leeds was such an avalanche of hard work that I hardly had time to eat.
>
> At present I am deeply interested in all the official efforts to deal with the poor and afflicted. This morning I was reading St. Luke 14:12 seq. It steadied my poor mind. Poor Law Reports are of another interest after reading Our Blessed Lord's words.[94]
>
> I am busy beyond words. From morning till night, I am unceasingly at work. Fr. Placid and Fr. Anselm are both away. Most of the parochial work drops on my shoulders. Thank God I sleep at nights. I never break into my rest if possible. If I did, the result would be immediate and decisive.[95]

And as Fr. Valentine continues:

> Those few extracts, chosen out of many, give some idea of the way he drove himself during those years. In the midst of all this work he found time to prepare his theses

> for his *Ad Gradus* examination in Rome when he had an audience with the Pope.[96]

Father Vincent authored more than thirty-five books over the course of his life (a number of them were compilations of essays previously written or retreat notes), in addition to giving retreats, teaching classes to Dominicans in formation, serving as a prior and a parish priest, engaging in public debates, preparing for his weekly audience at the Catholic Evidence Guild at Hyde Park, alongside impromptu and scheduled appearances at a number of the other open-air forums in and around London. He taught at Oxford one summer, was a guest host for the B.B.C. during the War, and was a regular contributor to several newspapers (both of these efforts will be addressed later).

But there is one effort above all that seemed nearest to his heart, the weekly *Summa* study he conducted every week for twenty-two years. This study was so dear to him that he missed only five times in the course of all those years. Miss Dorothy Finlayson describes the situation this way:

> In all those twenty-two years he missed only five lectures. He accepted no engagements which would prevent his being at his class. Often, he would cut short a retreat by one night, or make a special journey to town and back in order to keep his appointment with his students. Many times, he dragged himself down, on foot, from the Priory to Westminster when far stronger men would have allowed themselves to remain on a sick bed.[97]

All of the above was in addition to his great demand as a confessor, going out many mornings with Communion for the sick, instructing converts and all of those many activities he did in humble quiet, unbeknownst to his brethren. This level of activity kept up his entire life. It was simply his devotion, and a work ethic, no doubt inspired by the example of his parents, who had to provide for and take care of eleven children.

In terms of his outsize level of activity, it could even be evident in his walking. A woman retreatant describes the following:

> I remember the last retreat he gave at the Cenacle, Grayshott. The "Black-Out" was on then [during WWII], and as no car was at the station to meet him, he walked alone from Haselmere Station to the convent, a matter of six miles, in the pitch dark, without a torch, and he was then over seventy-one years of age. During the retreat, at times he seemed to be oblivious to those around him, and by watching the expression on his face, one could almost imagine he could see Heaven.[98]

And there was also this, from Fr. Valentine:

> But certainly Father Vincent did the oddest things, at least by our pedestrian standards. I remember once looking through the window of the Studentate at Hawkesyard when he was Prior and seeing him in the middle distance coming through the gate into the Priory quadrangle pushing a wheelbarrow piled high with books. On the top of the books was a black coat; on top of that a Roman collar. It was a very warm day and the Prior looked very hot indeed. As well he might, for he had set out several hours earlier to collect a number of old and precious books from some salesroom at Lichfield, six miles away. Alone he had trundled that wheelbarrow to and through Lichfield and alone he had trundled it all the way back. Perhaps you may not consider that very odd. You may argue as he did, when upbraided by the Fathers, that he needed the exercise, that he had saved the expense of having the books delivered and that the example of a young Prior of fifty exercising his body might encourage the rest of the community to open their pores by doing a little digging in the garden. Or again you might say that St. Philip Neri did still more alarming things, or that, for all his eccentricities, Fr. McNabb never tried to live on top of the pole like St. Simeon Stylites or to live on grass like the Cure of Ars.[99]

There is more to his walking than mere transport. It is clear that walking, for Father Vincent, was contemplation. Who has not sought the refuge of a walk to sort out thoughts, to pray or to simply be free? I am guessing on those walks he honed arguments, begged mercy, prayed for souls, gave thanks, and sought illumination. Those things typified his life. While his brethren may have seen inefficiency or foolishness,

Father Vincent surely saw opportunity, a rhythm to pray his fifteen-decade rosary daily, or as a way to simply be alone with the God he was wholly devoted to. At his core—and by his core is meant his *soul*—his full embrace of the miracle of life powered him forward. He moved those feet to the point of exhaustion because God had given them to him.

✠

But perhaps my favorite story of his varied ministry is the following. It speaks to his bravery, his great love for souls, his ability to relate to and inspire common people, his walking in the footsteps of St. Dominic, and his willingness to work to the point of exhaustion. It is told by Tom O'Brien, a Member of Parliament from a working-class background, who followed Father Vincent, notebook in hand, around London for more than a decade. Tom revered Father Vincent and his personal account of what Father Vincent meant to him is insightful and indicative of how many felt about the beloved friar. This is Tom's story of a night, years earlier:

> We are told that on one occasion St. Dominic stayed up all night debating with an apostate innkeeper until finally he had convinced him the error of his ways. I was reminded of this one day during the War [WWII]. The Blitz had descended upon us; and with some friends I had started a discussion group Friday in the back room of this pub and invited various prominent men to come and address us. Each lecture was followed by a discussion.
>
> ... One day I conceived the idea of asking Father Vincent to speak to us. I told several of the regulars about my plan, much to their amusement. What amused them was not that a priest should come to our local, though that was intriguing enough, but that a man like Father Vincent could pretend to have anything in common with ordinary folk who had little or no use for religion. Anyhow the majority of them agreed it would be rather fun, though they doubted he would accept my invitation.
>
> Father Vincent not only accepted but at 7:30 on the appointed evening he walked into the Freemasons Arms clad in his black and reasonably white habit, black-green

> hat and clod-hopping boots. Under his black Cappa he carried an old knapsack, the contents of which I did not see, but which I believe usually contained a Bible and odds and ends of notes. I took charge and steered him through the bar-parlour into the back room beyond. The others, mostly professional men—eighty to a hundred of them—followed carrying their drinks. As there was little seating accommodation, most of them stood, filling every inch of available space.
>
> What these fellows expected I do not know. But I'm sure they thought that this strange creature-relic of the Middle Ages would take a well-prepared manuscript out of his knapsack and dish up a lot of pious platitudes. I shall always remember his first words. As he stood before them, he said (rather grimly, I thought): "And now, gentlemen, what shall we talk about?"
>
> That in itself was something of a challenge. But after a brief pause one or two of the intellectuals spoke up and suggested—"The Problem of Evil"; and the majority of those present agreed. There was something rather topical about this debating point, in view of the blackout, bombing and destruction all around us; though I rather suspect those who suggested it—agnostics for the most part—were anxious to recapture the initiative. Anyhow, Father Vincent agreed to their choice of subject and stood there and talked for the best part of an hour, whilst the rest of them sipped their drinks and filled the room to suffocating with tobacco smoke.[100]

Father Vincent took on their questions, which generally centered around the feeling that God, if he existed, had abandoned humanity. He turned, naturally, those questions on their head. Mr. O'Brien noted Father Vincent saying (much as is the case in our own times) that

> he found one thing rather odd about this question, which so many were asking at the time. Why was it that when the world had abandoned God as a superfluous, old-time myth that it began to blame Him for the mess it had got itself into?
>
> . . . Many folk nowadays accepted the statements such as "there is no God" or "Religion is unreasonable and unnecessary," as dogmas accepted on the authority of

> the so-called leaders of modern thought. Education had dispensed with the need for believing in a divine Law-giver. God had been a convenient and useful hypothesis, but He had lost all meaning in this enlightened age.
>
> And now—lo and behold!—after undermining the laws of the Creator these people have the effrontery to complain when things go wrong with the world—"There you are!" they say. "What about your Christian God? Is he Almighty and All-good to let all this happen?"
>
> ... After his lecture Father Vincent asked me to come outside for a breath of fresh air, as he wasn't accustomed to inhaling tobacco smoke. We walked around for a few minutes whilst the company replenished their glasses at the bar. He talked to me, I remember, of Hitler, the War, and just how difficult it was going to before the nations to settle down to a just peace when it was all over. Then we returned to the Freemasons' Arms [N.B. there is something symbolic in the pub's name, of course] for "Question Time." He stayed with us that evening until 10:30, leaving our group of ordinary, if hard-boiled, professional men, a good deal wiser and certainly more respectful.[101]

Mr. O'Brien also had the following to say, an apt summary of a soul who was so influenced:

> I went to hear him preach on numerous occasions from the beginning of the 30s 'til his death in 1943. My personal reaction to him was something I could never quite analyse. I suppose it was the magnetic influence of his colourful personality. At least partly that. But fundamentally one knew intuitively that here at least was one man in London who practiced what he preached and radiated Christ. Even when he was tired—and at times he looked utterly exhausted—one felt he had spent himself for souls.
>
> I followed him all round London with notebook and pencil ... I not only went to any Church in which he was billed to preach, but would also go to Parliament Hill Fields or Marble Arch to hear him at the Catholic Evidence Guild pitch. Sometimes I walked back [to the Dominican Priory] with him, and it is no exaggeration to say that these were among the most thrilling moments of my life. During these tramps he would discuss many things in his impersonal way. Again and again he would repeat that he was no politician but a simple priest fighting to shape a

country fit for ordinary Christian men and women to live in. He deplored the wastage of things in our industrialized society in relation to man's body and soul. Perhaps, on reflection, that sums up the influence he wielded over so many of us. His diagnosis of our social ills was right and final. He had to get this across to ordinary folk, and this he did by insisting again and again on the principles contained in Rerum Novarum and by so explaining them that all could understand.

... For all is odd ways, I thank God every day of my life for the example and teaching of Father Vincent. I had not been given the advantage of a modern education ... but I sat at his feet week by week, [and] followed him all over London. I took shorthand notes copied these all out in longhand, pondering over what he had said and recalling the way he said it. I think I can truly say that I have grasped and tried to live by the principle he never tired of repeating—"To put first things first."[102]

Dominicans live, in a way, the best of both worlds for religious. They are both contemplative and active in the world. There is a deep focus on prayer as the basis for their lives, but unlike their purely monastic brethren, the Friars are called to share their faith with the world more overtly through preaching. This suited Father Vincent perfectly. From an early age, he was not just attuned to his faith, but was a debater. He would debate fellow students at St. Malachy's in Belfast and once they surrendered, he would offer to switch sides, and would win that side, too.[103] My great-grandfather tells a humorous story of Joe's combativeness when he was just thirteen, which would have been 1881. There was a debate in the kitchen of their home amongst the McNabb boys centered around how the just-assassinated American President Garfield would be replaced. Patrick writes:

> Joe, who had been listening to this conversation, suddenly piped in and said, "Oh! I could be President of the United States of America." . . . We all told Joe in unmistakable terms to shut up, which he refused to do, but kept repeating, "yes, I could, I could, I could. Finally, one of [us] brothers gave him a tiny slap on the face and Joe made the most of it. My father came rushing into the kitchen: 'What is going on here?" he called out in an angry voice. "Did anyone hit Joseph? Who was it?" Whoever it was that administered the blow spoke up and explained to my father what had led to it. Joe had said, he was told, that he could be President of the United States of America, even after his brother George had explained to him that

> the President of the United States had to be born in that country. My father then turned to us and said: "Did any of you ask him his reasons for making that claim? He must have had a reason." Of course, none of us had. So, turning to Joe, my father said: "You could not be President of the United States, Joe, for you have not been born in that country. Why do you say you could?" Then Joe replied, a little far-fetched perhaps, "I could, if God willed it."[104]

Father Vincent, ever the believer.

Along the lines of the believer and the brave debater, the following demonstrates both. A common theme of the time—and this spans the period of our entire human existence, of course (when will we learn, never?)—was the lament that God, if he even existed at all, was either not as benevolent as purported, given the sufferings of humanity, or that He didn't care, or perhaps was incapable of doing anything about it. Like today, where many have thrown support, full-thrust, to political solutions to society's ills. Politicians and radicals propose purely human solutions, and so many merely fall in line, backing the notion of a secular humanism that is just another form of Communism. It is back today with a vengeance, though very many well-intentioned people do not see it as such. Father Vincent did his part to address this. Siderman tells the following story:

> Fr. McNabb, being an Irishman and true to his race, loved an argument, and therefore it is not surprising that, when challenged to a debate, as he often was, he accepted if were at all possible ... A debate had been arranged to take place on a Sunday evening in the half of Battersea Baths, in South London, between Father Vincent and a member of the Communist Party. This affair was advertised in the *Daily Herald* ... .It was a very crowded meeting and judging by the applause the participants received when they appeared on the platform, the majority were there to support the Communist. Nevertheless, when Father Vincent appeared, in his well-known Dominican habit, and the inevitable shapeless hat and old boots, he also

> received a burst of applause, whether in support or derision it is impossible to say.
>
> The Communist spoke first ... [attacking] the Church on many grounds. He received a huge burst of applause as he sat down ... When Father Vincent rose to reply, there was a slight cheer from the people of the audience. He had a grim look on his face, and it was evident that he was aroused. Speaking without notes, he gave a general resume of the Church's teaching on social problems, and the relevant parts of *Rerum Novarum* [addressing the day's problems, and included statistics from a report from the Ministry of Health, and proposed "vivid illustrations" as to how these challenges could be addressed.]

But it was the underlying that he sought to address. The mighty scourge that plagued then, as now: a lack of understanding, and a lack of belief. Siderman continues:

> Then, walking to the front of the platform with his arms raised, speaking loudly, he asked, "Who has created these terrible conditions? Did almighty God, who made our beautiful Hampstead Heath, create these hovels?—No!—It is *man*, glorious *man*, who has been responsible for all these disgraceful conditions." Then picking up his haversack he dipped into it, and without further ado, walking to the front of the platform, he flung handfuls of leaflets to the audience. "Read these for yourselves!" he shouted with every fresh handful. It was evident he had stirred his audience, and there was a scramble to pick up the leaflets.
>
> Addressing his remarks to his opponent and to his audience, he said he regretted he could not stay any longer. He had already spoken and preached quite a lot that day, including his usual visit to Hyde Park, and he had to get back to the Priory. As he left, a part of the audience rose and cheered him.[105]

As insightful as this story is, it leaves a pain in the heart at the state of things today, at the dearth of voices within the Church to counter the onslaught of those seeking purely human solutions to our self-inflicted ills.

✠

I received an email today from the papal charity, *Aid to the Church in Need*. In it, the devastating situation in Lebanon was addressed. Among other things, the email stated: "There is no banking. People don't write checks and are incapable of cashing them. Bank accounts are inaccessible or frozen with minimum withdrawal allowances." I am reminded of how much more valuable "real" wealth versus "token" wealth can be; "things," as Father Vincent would say, versus "tokens of things." I do not mean to exploit the sufferings of the Lebanese to explain a point, but like a man stranded in a desert, a cup of water is much more valuable than a brick of gold. Sometimes (and increasingly), I am filled with the unease that this plight that Lebanon (and other countries) are experiencing, is destined, too, for the rest of us.

✠

Father Vincent was skeptical of new technology, and the related enabling of the "token." He would often say the two words that frightened him the most were "efficiency" and "progress", "because of the dangers which he said were inherent in them, and of which he had warned people, who seemed to him to be either oblivious of the dangers or seemed to think that he was just a scaremonger out of touch with modern life and conditions."[106]

He remarked once, in tones of bitter sarcasm, that we were heading for a time with "Slot machines all over the place; soon you will be able to have your nose blown for you by putting a coin in a slot machine."[107] And while there could be much more said about all this, as I sit here and write this in Portland, Maine, I have in the background on my computer a live webcam of the sanctuary of St. Patrick's church in Portaferry, the very place that was so dear to him and his family, where he was baptized and offered up to St. Joseph. It is remarkable. And it is beautiful. And I am grateful for this. But I am not unsympathetic to the dehumanizing ends for which so much of our "progress" is aimed. In this, *St. Patrick, pray for us! St. Joseph, pray for us!*

✠

My family is far from perfect, but we are, by and large, faithful. Raising our children in the faith has not been difficult at all, and I am reminded of Jesus's words, "My yoke is easy, my burden light." What *is* a challenge, however, is raising faithful children amidst the culture. They have mobile phones. They are not homeschooled. They attend a secularized Catholic high school, which is probably the greatest challenge of all; what we accept in a secularized culture is difficult to countenance when embraced by a school with a Catholic charter. There is a temptation to withdraw, to circle the wagons, but that doesn't seem to be our calling. We stay, and we witness. And we are human, of course. My kids, like their parents, and, indeed, like all of humanity, are flawed. We can always do better.

In this regard, it is heartening to read Father Vincent's words about his own family, particularly these:

> I love to go back in my memory and see the working of a normal Catholic family—a family that put God first. There was hardly any piety—thank God!—but we were in Northern Ireland where you had to fight for your Faith—and what piety we had was kept up and treasured—the first thing in life.
>
> ... Some member of my family was at daily Mass every morning—usually two or three of us. If anyone was not awake [on Sundays] the others would say "Not up yet!" and off came the bedclothes. We cheerfully made each other get up. That was a large family! I was brought up in an atmosphere of cheerful Sundays—toffee you made yourself. Holy Mass was the centre of the day—and love of it was in your very blood.[108]

His mention of there being hardly any piety is encouraging. I think what he is saying is that theirs was not a house of ready-made saints. There were so many of them, and the boys in particular were boisterous, and frequently got in trouble (particularly when their father was away at sea). They were, in other words, a normal family. A normal *Catholic* family. My family is no different, except in number. We fight amongst ourselves. We say uncharitable things. There have been a few problems with behavior at school. We, as I said, can always do better. But, I am proud to say, God is put first. When we transgress, we recognize it. We make amends. And our Sunday obligation is always kept, and the day is made to feel special. Quite naturally, many graces have flown from this.

Father Vincent's referencing the situation in Ulster being difficult for Catholics is also reassuring. Though there are essential differences between that and the present environment, a hostility to the faith is the commonality. Perhaps the difference is in overtness. While the hostility is sometimes overt, the greater danger is in the apathy, in the lukewarmness of people of faith and the outright indifference of so many others—friends, acquaintances. The rise of the "Nones," in contemporary society, if you will. With regard to my children and the temptations of the culture, coming to mind is the title of that great Cranberries album, "If Everyone Else is Doing It, Why Can't We?"

Given where they are in their lives, so prone to the influence of others, the concept of heroic virtue enters once again. As Fr. Vincent was quick to point out, it was those situations where the average person—which is to say, most of us—must exhibit not just regular virtue, but heroic virtue to keep from sin. He referenced that mostly in terms of the economic environment of the time that was changing how people lived, but today it is simply *the* environment. I know sin deeply, unfortunately. I also know of His mercy and forgiveness for a contrite soul, thankfully. And I pray for my children's purity as we raise them amidst the culture.

✠

In light of our troubled times, we hear increasingly about Our Lady of Fatima. I do not know what Father Vincent thought about the apparitions, particularly in light of information and revelations being revealed over the ensuing decades, and greatly after Father Vincent had passed. One thing for certain, akin to subsequent revelations, is adequately summed up by

Mr. Bryan Keating, secretary of the Catholic Land Movement, who wrote that Father Vincent "saw with Apocalyptic clearness of vision that the most formidable attack the Church faced today was the attack on family life."[109]

Two of the three visionaries died in childhood. The third, Lucia dos Santos, would become a Carmelite nun, Sr. Lucia. Over the course of her long life, she continued to be given further understanding and expansion of the visions she experienced as a child. While there is some mystery to this, and we do not know all that may have been revealed to her, perhaps the most poignant subsequent revelation was divulged by Cardinal Carlo Caffarra, who had read a handwritten letter from Sr. Lucia to St. Pope John Paul II in the early 1980s. The letter ended with the words, "Father, a time will come when the decisive battle between the kingdom of Christ and Satan will be over marriage and the family. And those who will work for the good of the family will experience persecution and tribulation. But do not be afraid, because Our Lady has already crushed his head."

Prophetic, indeed, and not surprising at all that Father Vincent recognized the family—*Nazareth*—was under attack, and thus he did all he could to warn, combat, and give hope.

In this regard, *Sr. Lucia, pray for us! Father Vincent, pray for us! Mother Mary, protect us!*

WE HEAR, today, about a contraceptive mentality; a divorcing of the sexual act from procreation. At least in Catholic circles. We are even being told contraception is "responsible." Our houses, at least in America, are bigger, our families, smaller. The birth rate in the West is below replacement. The Pope, though sometimes sending mixed messages, recently implored the Italians to have more children. The Chinese have just woken to the fact that they are facing a population cliff given their years of forced abortions and contraception. Still, and incredibly, *Humanae Vitae* is under attack, even within the Church. By some accounts, as many as ninety percent of Catholic couples use birth control, which is often used as an argument in favor. Siderman, in a memorable quote, recounts Father Vincent going apoplectic over an advertisement he had seen in the newspaper seeking young girls to work in a factory that produced birth control. He writes:

> One of the rare occasions on which I have seen Father McNabb really angry was when advertisements appeared in some newspapers offering employment to young girls at high wages, in factories, for the production of contraceptives. I do not ever remember him using such angry words of denunciation as he did on this matter. Stamping his feet on the platform, he said, "It's horrible, horrible, when one thinks of the effect of such employment on the minds of young girls. He denounced the authorities who were responsible for permitting these conditions to exist and also the newspapers for printing the advertisements.[110]

I was reminded of this last night when I was sitting on the couch with my fifteen-year-old daughter watching television around seven o'clock. An advertisement came on. A lone hand grasping at a silky sheet, we both soon realized, in sexual ecstasy. Then came the tag line, about a condom. I glanced over at my daughter; the embarrassment on her face. It is just as Father Vincent noted, but instead of a young woman intentionally working in a factory, here there was no choice. The innocence sadly fades, out from the factories, and into the family room.

✠

Part of this could be attributed to the sexual revolution. That did not start, apparently, in the 1960s, but was gaining traction decades prior. Father Vincent, in one of his most memorable lines shouted from the platform of the Catholic Evidence Guild, is recounted by Siderman,

> When asked about "Free Love," he almost exploded with indignation. "The Catholic Church has the only Free Love! Outside the Church Free Love means Animal Licence. It is degrading men and women below the animals," and his voice was vitriolic as he gave his reply.[111]

✠

Yes, Father Vincent was known to make statements that would shock. Mostly, this was unintentional and was due to, as Fr. Hilary Carpenter's described it, Father Vincent's "uncompromising sincerity, which stood out so forcibly in an age so much contributed to what is sham and unreal."[112] He simply spoke the truth. Sometimes the truth is shocking. In all ages, men are lowly and bring shame upon themselves. In all ages, prophetic voices are inspired to call out that which is "sham and unreal." And in our own time? The artifice is blatant. Where are the voices? There are not as many, perhaps, but they are here. If you are listening.

And in this regard, he held in high regard, unsurprisingly, St. Thomas Aquinas. These words of Father Vincent are particularly relevant:

> As a student of St. Thomas Aquinas, I had not failed to notice his genius, not only for refusing to create new words, but also for using the old words in their old traditional meaning. I had long been perplexed by the quick changes that modern social activities had been affecting on old words, such as reason, food, faith, justice, charity, etc. The word MARRIAGE especially perplexed me.
>
> Finding myself lately with two of the leading juniors in the Divorce Court, I asked point blank: "Could you give me the present definition of MARRIAGE in English Law?"[113]

Father Vincent goes on to recount the fumbling of the two, stating, "I was not prepared for their hesitation in answering such a simple, relevant official question."[114] And that was then. What would it be today? I don't think even Fr. Vincent, in all his prophetic wisdom, could have foreseen the situation today.

I just looked up the phrase New Words on the internet. Merriam Webster stated they had added 370 words to their dictionary in September 2022 alone. My favorite among them? *Virtue signaling*. In our age of sermonizing through bumper stickers and yard signs, not all new words are bad, I guess.

But now turning to lighter fare, as already mentioned, despite the challenges of the times, Father Vincent was an incredibly joyful man. This makes sense. On that most elemental level—and he was elemental; let us not forget his focus on primary things, the simplicity of his life, the bareness of his cell, his disregard (in the best sense of the word) for his personal appearance—he understood Jesus had come to redeem man and thereby make everything right, to make possible that only good end: eternal bliss. When this knowledge is never far from a soul's awareness, joy becomes a *habit.*

Though his biographer goes into great detail about Father Vincent's lifelong confliction, his feeling unworthy of this most tremendous gift, "the plight of his own soul in search of humility and a happy death,"[115] his desire for progress in the spiritual life and God's grace ultimately won out. The holy soul will not succumb to the darkness of negativity or doubt for long.

The holy soul recognizes his own deficiencies, and the great need for God's mercy, of course. But the holy soul will be elevated by the Holy Spirit. The holy soul, in being given the gifts of the Holy Spirit, will, despite difficulties, trials and challenges, recognize *he … is … saved,* and a natural joy will exude. After all, what more can be hoped for? Temporal satisfaction, as well, of course. But the worthy and illuminated soul recognizes the vicissitudes of life, the *need* for suffering, and the benefits of such, and that all things are grace. Father Vincent's book, *The Craft of Suffering,* is an explication of such.

For him, despite whatever self-doubts or inner confliction he suffered, joy was, in fact, a habit. This made its way into his everyday interactions, and in his outlook. Even when he was ill with the throat cancer that would bring his end, he was determined to not be, as he said, a "wet blanket."

✠

And speaking of joy. I took a walk today, and it was good. So very, very good. It was just from my house to the intersection of the major avenue a mile away. It, to most eyes, would be an unremarkable walk in a non-descript section of this small city. Sidewalked, which is nice. But just a walk. If there is such a thing. But I don't believe there is, actually. Any walk on its own, under God's sky, recommends itself. The miracle of the foot, as Father Vincent would say.

And while this particular walk is, in many ways, unremarkable, there is the breath of life as it is lived in taking the same walk frequently. The subtle differences of day to day, week to week. The leaves up or down, the fleeting detritus, the habits of the cars in driveways, the shades in windows, and the head nods to the occasional person. Simple things. Simple, beautiful things.

✠

I must admit, though, there are times in my life, particularly when I think of the level of industriousness and indefatigability Father Vincent displayed, that I feel I am coming up short or I am not as productive as I could be, that I am not tilling the fields I have been given. I will refer to the point of the previously mentioned economist Thomas Woods, who made the claim that one of the benefits of capitalism and efficiency was that there is more leisure time. I will echo part of my response to that, that this leisure time, today, is largely spent not well. While I would never say I am a layabout—I most certainly am not—I do have more time for pondering *greater things* than most (and this was part of Woods's point). This is due to my wife's own industriousness in her effort to support this family of six, and the grace and blessings of God to enable me to do what I do. But still.

Am I doing all I can? Am I doing God's will? This particular anecdote from a letter written by a woman who greatly admired Father Vincent gives insight into his respect for the domestic church and makes me feel heartened by the work I do to keep my four children heading in the right direction: up.

> I am a member of the Aquinas Society, and once I called on him [Father Vincent] to ask him to explain something about which my husband and a clever philosopher friend were arguing. He gave me the answer, and then he asked me about myself. I told him I was a grannie of six. He then said, "Why come to meet me? You are the greater philosopher because you have done something, and I have only talked."
>
> After that, whenever he wrote to me he always began, "Dear Grannie Philosopher." What a wonderful man he was, and what a wonderful face he had.[116]

One could never say Father Vincent had "only talked," or that his "talking" was not fruitful, but it is his respect for family life—for Nazareth—that so shines through. That he would elevate this grandmother, and refer to her not just as a grannie, but a Truth-seeking grannie and thus a grannie philosopher says everything about how he respected family life. Should I think of myself, then, as Daddy Philosopher?

✠

Yes, Ann McNabb was famous for saying, "Eleven, thank God!" when asked how many children she had. Here is the list of their names, in order of birth. Mary, James, Margaret, Georgina, George Neil, Richard, John, Patrick, Laurence, Joseph (Father Vincent), and Annie (Sr. Mary Vincent).

Years ago, I learned from my spiritual director the Catholic practice of naming one's children lost through miscarriage. My wife and I subsequently did this. They are: Mary, Theresa, Catherine, Mercie, John, Peter and Paul. These are in addition to those who are now living in the world, Marina, Luke, Leo and

Hope. Together, this, too, makes eleven. So, I guess I, too, can say when asked how many children I have, "Eleven, Thank God!"

✠

I have been thinking a lot, lately, about the faith of Ann McNabb, my great-great grandmother. She, really, is the spiritual matriarch of these ensuing generations of McNabbs. Her own parents were devout souls, and well regarded in their native Rathmullan, Donegal. Of them, Father Vincent wrote, "in their old age, both [my grandfather] and my grandmother had such a reputation for charitable deeds (he was active in burying the cholera dead) that their priest, Fr. Marner, D.D., used to bring them Holy Communion regularly soon after midnight to prevent them fasting."[117]

Ann was nurtured, clearly, in an atmosphere of faith and her embrace of that and the gifts therein is evident. Her faith and indulgence of God's grace were inspiration in her turning her back on the American dream to return to Ireland for the sake of her soul. God had other plans for her. Her family and its legacy is affirmation of her decision.

My thoughts about Ann McNabb, on one hand, relate to family. It is no surprise that Father Vincent, reared in such a faith-filled and loving environment, was adamant about the sanctity and primacy of such. That is not a sentiment he devised on his own, of course, but that of the Church, which recognizes the family as the basic unit of society—the so-called *domestic church*. Yes, the Church begins at home, just as it is urged in Deuteronomy (6:4)—

> The Lord is our God, the Lord alone. Therefore, you shall love the LORD, your God, with your whole heart, and with your whole being, and with your whole strength. Take to heart these words I enjoin on you today. Drill them into your children. Speak of them at home and abroad, whether you are busy or at rest.

—because the home is where life necessarily takes root.

The domestic church from which Ann hailed was strong in faith and morals, and she brought that to her own family, and that has cascaded the generations. I consider myself and my family direct beneficiaries. This faith, inculcated through a literal handing down of practice and education, but also by the grace of God's continued blessing on those who remain faithful alongside the intercession of those family members who have earned their place in the communion of saints. In light of this, it is no wonder that Satan seeks the destruction of the family and deludes those who are seeking upheaval today in seeking to bring about a new vision for society an updated morality, and are intent on dismantling the traditional family. And it is no wonder that we are in such a state today given the family's disintegration.

But my thoughts about Ann McNabb have also turned to her faith, her conviction, and most of all, her trust. Trust, for me, has always been difficult. Not that I don't trust, at least intellectually, but what trust calls for—action but relenting, action but giving over, action but acceptance—has always been a challenge.

There are those family stories that carry on, and certainly Ann's leaving New York is seminal, but no less powerful is her fortitude and trust apparent than in the previously given account of the sailor on the boat on which Ann gave birth to George Neil off the west coast of South America. That she even embarked on this two-year journey at sea with her husband demonstrates devotion and fortitude, but when my great-great-grandfather, James, the captain of the vessel, had urged her, some time before she gave birth at sea, to stay on at New Zealand and he would pick her up on his way back, the following was her response:

> "No, James," she said, "I will go with you. God will provide."
>
> The first mate used to describe what happened in his own way: "Well," he would say, "I don't believe in God or the Devil. But the day that child was born was a miracle. There had been storms for weeks before; there were storms for weeks after. But the day the child was born, the Pacific was as calm as a mill pond!"

Again, there was not another woman on the boat. And let us

be clear, this was not a big boat and she, in the late stages of pregnancy, must have been incredibly uncomfortable. Her ability to absorb the discomfort was surely a guidepost for her own children, Father Vincent in particular given his intentional self-deprivations. He, unsurprisingly, employed the spiritual adage, *Trust as if everything depends on God, and work as if everything depends on you,* a number of times to describe his mother's approach. I can imagine her never being too distraught at plans not working out or working out differently than she had imagined. I desire that for myself. I try to trust, and I do, sometimes, but that second part, that working hard as if everything depends on me, often wins out, and I forget about the former, which is much more important. It can be dispiriting.

Finally, I am reminded of her name, Ann. It is not lost on me, that this spiritual grandmother shares the name of Jesus's grandmother. Here again, is the beauty of the faith. Here again, is the power of tradition, of biblical names, of their evocations. Father Vincent's given name was Joseph. He was given this name and was also offered, formally, to St. Joseph, and many times throughout his life he and his mother called out for that powerful saint's intercession.

And in this regard, I pray now, *St. Anne, and great-great-grandmother Ann McNabb, pray for us!*

✠

And speaking of St. Anne … and walking, the ability to walk is often taken for granted. My two daughters were late to walking. Each suffered a stroke in-utero. An unusual way to come into the world. Only God knows why. The gift of suffering, perhaps. The gift of example for others? Definitely. They both have cerebral palsy and are heroic. My elder daughter never crawled. This, we are told, has contributed to other issues. But her first steps were a joyous, joyous occasion. It was (and is) treacherous, though. She grew up on brick sidewalks and not a lot of green (sorry, Father Vincent). After-dinner walks were a bruised and bleeding adventure. My girls walk differently. There is the drop toe. The arm up. There are the nighttime orthotics. The daytime lifts. The pending surgeries. To walk. Watching them is watching the joy of the will and of human triumph.

But there is pain, still. For them. For my wife and me. For their healing, we went on a pilgrimage to the shrine of St. Anne de Beaupre in Quebec. The shrine was built by devout French Canadians to counter the number of shipwrecks on the St. Lawrence River. St. Anne is the patron saint of sailors, and they sought her protection. I am sure the seafaring McNabb family had a devotion to her as well.

Our trip was a beautiful one; unequivocally the best and most enjoyable trip I have taken in my life. I believe my wife and children think so, too. That the pillars at the entrance to the basilica are covered with crutches, canes and braces representing those that have been healed is almost beside the point.

✠

And speaking of death ... Well, actually, we don't speak of death that much anymore, do we? Or when we do it is as an incomparable tragedy. And sometimes death is tragic. And in those times, it is even more evident to me that this life is not all there is to our existence. When one has a proper understanding of life, one has a proper understanding of death. Father Vincent, of course, had a proper understanding of both. But with regard to the latter, and thus not unrelated to the former, later in life he writes:

> I sometimes wonder of those who have heard the word of death spoken to them and have accepted its message, ever quite realise what they have given to the priest of God who has been privileged to serve them ...[118] Our Lord's death seems to me to answer all difficulties. I question whether there is a priest in England who has heard more difficulties than I. The answer to all is the answer of death. They move me to pity and if they seem to move my mind, I have the answer of death beneath my scapular [the crucifix.] I take into my hands the figure of my saviour crucified. If that does not answer, there is no other answer.[119]

The answer to death: Christ. How so? Those sorrowful souls, pitiable and seeking mercy. I am reminded of Jesus who, "At the sight of the crowds, his heart was moved with pity for them because they were troubled and abandoned, like sheep without a shepherd" (Matthew 9:36). And in that moment Jesus became their shepherd. And he said to his disciples, "The harvest is abundant, but the laborers are few; so ask the master of the harvest to send out laborers for his harvest" (Matthew 9:37–8). And here was Father Vincent, the laborer, so, as he said, privileged. Privileged to be reminded of the grace of death. Privileged to be acting *in persona Christi*, ministering to the sorrowful, pitiable souls. But most of all, privileged to know of that greatest privilege, that in Christ's death we have the answer to death: life.

He writes often of death, of its illumination, and one of the more touching accounts relates to his brother, Laurence:

> I often recount the death of a beloved brother [Laurence], a doctor. He had such intelligence I think he was able to tell every avenue of pain. When death came to him, the father of seven children, he greeted it in a most courteous manner with "Thanks be to God. Thanks be to God." The thought of every child he was leaving must have wrung his heart but once the call from God came to part with the little world that was all the world to him, for home was his world, there was just the sense of God's great gift, and He could only be thanked for that. Few of the memories of my life are quite so treasured.[120]

Yes, the affirmation of Laurence's last words, his being welcomed into that beatific vision. If you have a proper understanding of death, then this is what is possible—and that it is not guaranteed—then you will have the proper understanding of life.

A remarkable and telling instance of this being rooted in him from an early age occurred when he was a boy of twelve, and his sister, Margaret, was dying. My great-grandfather Patrick tells the following story:

> For weeks he had been spending time in the sickroom, reading to his sister from religious books. Not many

days before the end, I was in the back parlour doing my homework, I think, conscious of the fact that Joe and mother were upstairs in the sick room, when suddenly the door opened, and my mother came in. She drew a chair up close to mine and with much feeling she said: "Patrick, that boy Joseph gives me more consolation than I can express in words. As we sat in the sick room just now, before the open fire, talking quietly about Maggie, who had fallen asleep, I said to him: 'Son, it is very hard to lose Maggie right now that she has grown up and after she has weathered three or four illnesses. She ought to have many pleasant years ahead of her. Don't you think she deserves to recover?'"

Then my mother turned to me and said, "Patrick, do you know what the boy said to me?" I shook my head. "He said, 'Mother, Maggie has suffered much from her previous illnesses and from this one, too. In a few days her sufferings will be over and she will certainly receive her reward for them in Heaven. Now, Mother, would you really want to bring her back to good health so that she would have to go through all the pains of approaching death once again?'"[121]

Such wisdom and understanding at such a young age.

I must say, death is never far from my mind. Not always in the best sense, but mostly. I ended my short story collection, *The Body of This*, with the following brief piece, *It's Time to Die*.

Okay already, let's just make it time to die. I am forty. I am a believer in the good Lord, God and in Jesus Christ, His only Son, who died on the cross for my sins and the sins of mankind. So, why not?

I have told my wife, "Life is like a prolonged finals week, don't you just want to be on summer vacation?"

She has always replied, "God gave us this life not just to die, but to live."

"That's true," I said one time, "but Jesus was only thirty-three."

"Moses was over a hundred," she answered.

I almost told her that I have always found that hard to believe—because why would I, if I believed all of the other stuff?—but I just kept my trap shut.

I go on living, of course. And no, nothing is so bad:

> American. Or maybe it's too, too bad: American, or just plain human.
>
> But anyway, no one can see inside my mind where I wonder, still, *Why can't it just be time to die?*[122]

And perhaps echoing this, I was amused to read Father Vincent's words, "We must go on. I hope to die going on. I would be almost pleased if one day walking back to St. Dominic's I died in the street."[123]

Both accounts are more mirthful than wishful, but reflect an understanding of the goodness and relief of what comes next.

As previously mentioned, of the many notable efforts in Father Vincent's varied ministry, one that was particularly fruitful was his work for Christian unity. As learned as he was, as devout as he was, as firm as he was in his understanding of the fullness of Truth residing in the Catholic faith, he gave great respect to other Christians in their efforts in seeking Him. There was humility in this, and, ultimately, a simple but deep desire for God to be reverenced and loved.

This is all the more remarkable as he was an Ulsterman, and had experienced the prejudices of Protestants, not to mention that as a moral theologian and a deft apologist, he could easily refute arguments against the Catholic faith. He did this when appropriate, of course; there were many battles in this regard waged from the platform of the Catholic Evidence Guild, but even there, his tone was always cordial and his intent was education and illumination, not victory. This comment from Father Vincent himself speaks to this:

> A few nights ago, I had to have a discussion with a very calm and complete communist. Two small girls were standing spellbound, open-eyed and open-mouthed for half an hour or more. When I got down from the platform with "God bless you," to them all, one of the little ones said in a half-reassuring voice "You won!" That went through me like a knife. All I could do was put my hand on her head and say, "My little one. I don't want to win. I only want the truth to win."[124]

His understanding of the essence of life itself was deeper than the merely sectarian. He understood to be human is to be body and spirit, created by God in His image and likeness and, once created, to exist forever; our bodily existence comprised just a mite of "forever", but that that mite determined what "forever" would be. There was only one good outcome. He dedicated his life to ensuring his own outcome would be good and to influence as many others as he could in the same, owing everything to the munificence of our Creator, and to the redemption brought by the Creator's Only Son. Yes, he desired that everyone reside fully in the Catholic faith; but he sought to work with people where they were. In this, though, he was uncompromising in the primacy of the Catholic faith. He one time heard from a member of the audience that "One religion is as good as another" and greatly refuted him.[125] Seeking reconciliation and understanding among Christian brethren is admirable; today, that effort even within the Church too often flirts with descent into religious indifferentism, which is a heresy.

Having said that, as evidenced below, in working together there could be benefits to both Protestants and Catholics, and society in general. Siderman writes of Father Vincent's involvement with the ecumenical Public Morality Council:

> One Sunday afternoon arriving at the Speakers' Corner at Marble Arch I was surprised to see Fr. McNabb about to speak from the platform of the Public Morality Council, who usually held their meetings some little distance from where the Catholic Evidence Guild hold theirs. The Public Morality Council is an organization whose aim is the raising of the standard of morals of the individual and of the public, and to this end hold outdoor meetings in the parks and other places. The [Anglican] Bishop of London is the Chairman of the Council and the speakers are men of various religious denominations, and include parsons, doctors lawyers, welfare workers and sometimes a member of Parliament.[126]

Allow me to say how wonderful this is, in light of current

times, when ridicule would certainly be heaped on any attempt to address, in such a public way, the issue of public morals. Research shows the council was started in 1899 and ceased, perhaps unsurprisingly, in 1967 in the midst of the wreck being caused by the Sexual Revolution. Siderman continues,

> Their meetings in Hyde Park are well attended, and the chairman for many years and one of its regular and principal speakers was a Methodist minister, the Rev. George Kendal, O.B.E., a retired chaplain of His Majesty's Forces ... Although I had heard several parsons speaking on this platform, the sight of Fr. McNabb on it rather surprised and intrigued me, and I immediately went over to listen to him.
>
> There was a large crowd, which included many of the usual attendants at the Catholic Evidence Guild, Catholic and non-Catholic, who also were as surprised as I was, and has come to hear Father Vincent. Needless to say, on the question of morality as it concerned the individual and the public generally, he was an exceptionally good speaker and made a great impression on his audience. He began by pointing out that the Public Morality Council welcomed speakers from any denomination, that they were doing a good and vital work for the benefit of the Community and that he was grateful to them for the invitation to speak from their platform, and thought that Catholics should take their part in this necessary work. He was deeply concerned about the moral delinquency and sex licence especially among so many young people of today, and as there were always crowds of young people in the park he wanted to talk to them, their parents, and all grown-up people, because in the matter of the morality of the people, all were, or should be, concerned.
>
> [On that day and subsequent others at that forum], he would begin by saying, "I am a Catholic Priest and I have come to talk to you." He then took out his Bible from the familiar haversack and read the Ten Commandments or sometimes the Sermon on the Mount. Often when reading the Commandments, he would speak of Moses: "All men who love freedom and liberty, whose hearts are touched with compassion, who are fighting human wickedness, must find in him their ideal, for his law was pure. He laid the foundations for a glorious kingdom where equal

> rights and an ideal perfect freedom could be realised, He prepared the way for Christ."[127]

He would go on to speak for the Council on more occasions, most notably in 1936. Siderman recounts:

> The largest gathering Fr. McNabb ever addressed in Hyde Park took place in 1936. It was a great United Demonstration organized by the Rev. George Kendall, Mr. Crook Palmer [a Methodist], and Father Vincent McNabb ... an enormous crowd gathered to listen. The Catholic Evidence Guild, very wisely, had suspended its usual meeting, its speakers and audience joining with the others. Sir Thomas Moloney, a former Chief Justice of Ireland, himself a Catholic and Vice-Chairman of the Public Morality Council, was in attendance as were also leaders of the Salvation Army and Free Churches. When Fr. McNabb was called on to speak, he quickly mounted the platform and for a few seconds was prevented from speaking by the great reception with which the huge audience greeted him. On quietness being restored, he began by saying this was an historic occasion, as never before had Christians belonging to different denominations met together as they were now, in a common interest, and purpose, which was the raising and purification of the morals of the individual and the nation. He then proceeded to give a magnificent address, as only he could give it, and when it ended, the applause of the crowd left him in no doubt as to their appreciation of his efforts ... The Rev. George Kendal has told me some time prior to the United Demonstration, Mr. Crook Palmer, Father Vincent and himself had met together in a room at the Kingsway Hall, the Headquarters of the West London [Methodist] Mission, to discuss and make arrangements for the Demonstration ... After a long conversation on their plans, the three then knelt together in prayer. [Said, Rev. Kendall,] "It was like a real 'Upper Room' with the same atmosphere as on the Day of Pentecost. Two Methodists and a Catholic priest praying for the success of this meeting. No wonder it was a success."[128]

These were not his only efforts. In a letter to his brother Laurence, he writes of being invited by the Rev. Spencer Jones, of the Church of England, to give a talk about papal infallibility to the Society of Clergy and Laymen, a group formed to study relations between England and the Holy See. He was commended by the Anglican bishop, George Bell, who was also a proponent of Christian unity. In a letter to the prior at St. Dominic's in London, on the very date that Father Vincent died, Bishop Bell wrote:

> What a marvellous spirit he had; what an inspiration it was to be in his company, and read what he wrote and receive his letters. I remember so well his visit to Chichester [where he was bishop], now alas a few years ago. He did from time to time write to me in the kindest of terms. I know how ardent was his faith, and how passionate his desire for Christian unity.[129]

On another occasion, as previously written, Father Vincent told of a meeting he had had with the Anglican archbishop (the head of the worldwide Anglican communion) at Lambeth Palace. After talking for a long time, they knelt and prayed together. What a beautiful statement. What a moment. Father Vincent on his knees, praying beside the archbishop of Canterbury.

✠

At Father Vincent's funeral, clergy from various Protestant denominations were present, and one of the eulogists was the aforementioned Methodist minister, Rev. George Kendal, who offered the following poetic words (referencing Father Vincent's final visit to Speakers' Corner at Marble Arch just a few weeks earlier):

> Thousands had listened to him throughout the years, and especially during the war years; a common suffering had bound them to him by a thousand ties. He looked toward the Marble Arch; it was past. He looked forward to heaven; it was near. He turned to the people, and some were in tears. And then, as his voice—not the stirring voice of old, just a whisper, and the crowd straining their ears to catch every word—gave his final benediction, the silence could almost be felt.

> ... Our common humanity will find at Marble Arch a memorial more enduring than brass, whiter than marble, richer than gold. For here was a saint, who had sublime self-restraint with mighty passion, modest without loss of self-respect, humble without fear to face the cosmopolitan crowd, sometimes hostile but always won by his friendliness.
>
> His stature will grow more sublime with the years as glittering errors fade and Truth finds her home.[130]

His words are remarkable on several levels. First, the beauty of the tribute itself. Second, the beauty of the fruits of respect between men of different faith. And third, by yet another mention of the sublime sanctity of the Very Reverend Father Vincent McNabb, O.P.

✠

For Father Vincent, reaching across sectarian lines was not limited to fellow Christians. He had a deep love for the Jewish people. Viewing the world and the human race, as we have seen, by its roots and origins, he would naturally recognize the exalted position of the Jews and their role in salvation history. And beyond the obvious, Father Vincent frequently made the point, aligned with his penchant for "small" things or little groups that, "The Jews, like my own people, the Irish, were a little group."[131]

Indeed, it was E. A. Siderman, a Jew, who wrote the beautiful book about Father Vincent, *A Saint in Hyde Park*. In his introduction to the book, Frank Sheed writes:

> For over twenty years, Father Vincent McNabb, a Dominican Priest, spoke every Sunday afternoon from the platform of the Catholic Evidence Guild at Marble Arch, Hyde Park and on nearly each occasion his audience included Mr. Edward Siderman, an Orthodox Jew, who became Father Vincent's most persistent heckler ... Let no one think that being heckled by Mr. Siderman is fun. It is just about the most strenuous mental combat there is, and Father Vincent found it so. But this book could not have been written unless, in that long drawn-out battle, the heckler had grown to love the friar. I *know* the friar had grown to love the heckler.[132]

This book is stunning, not just in its account of Father Vincent over the decades (and from which I have drawn heavily to write this book), but that it was written with such humility by this Jewish man. This cannot be overstated. Siderman was a Jew. In his book, he writes with absolutely no prejudice of Father Vincent's Christian apologetics. Not only was there no prejudice or dismissal of that which would be contrary to his own beliefs, Siderman's demonstrated understanding of the subject matter is formidable and his embrace inspiring. The depth of their relationship is as much—or more—to be attributed to the character and humility of Mr. Siderman, as it is to Father Vincent.

I continue to be struck by the civility of the open-air forums of that time in light of today's unabated rancor and anti-intellectualism, where zingers and name-calling and "cancelling" rule. Not that there were not flared tempers or heckling at these forums, or that everyone demonstrated respect and open-mindedness and good-will. Indeed, Frank Sheed described the proceedings at Hyde Park as "not a school of courtliness," and there are many (often amusing) accounts of Father Vincent skillfully dealing with hecklers and difficult persons.

There were the infamous Screaming Jinny and Black Maria, who were as tough as they came (because they were not interested in true debate, but in the spectacle they could cause; Siderman had heard they were paid by a Protestant group to disrupt the proceedings), but the more common hecklers were no match for Father Vincent, who frequently tied them up in knots. One of my favorite encounters, told by Mr. Siderman, was this:

> Man: You say he came to forgive sin.
> Father Vincent: Yes
> Man: Then why didn't he come sooner?
> Father Vincent: Do you want your sins forgiven?
> Man: No
> Father Vincent: Then he didn't come too soon for you![133]

And there are many more accounts along these lines. But truth being sought so authentically in the form of debate must have been so hopeful. That actual dialogue was not just possible but encouraged and a part of the culture.

As for Siderman, Sheed describes his formidable intellect, but his genius, really, and the greatest aspect of his approach, was his ability *to listen.* In any event, of the many accounts of Father Vincent relating to the Jews, this from Siderman is both entertaining and affirming:

> A story Fr. McNabb delighted in telling us, was that one day when visiting parishioners in the back street of St. Pancras, one young urchin, seeing him (in his Dominican habit), shouted to his pals, "Look, boys, here comes old Gandhi!" And he told us of a similar instance when he was visiting the East End of London, and urchin upon seeing him, yelled, 'Ho, there is old Elijah!' Fr. McNabb said, "It made me feel very proud."
>
> Once when referring to the Old Testament, a young Jew said, "How can anyone believe in the Bible? It's all lies."
>
> Immediately Fr. McNabb retorted, "Well, if it is all lies, it was your ancestors who wrote it, so you are not paying your own people much of a compliment."
>
> Whereupon the Jew said, "I cannot help being born a Jew; I am not proud of it."
>
> At once Fr. McNabb replied, "Had I been born a Jew, I should be very proud of it. Our Lord was a Jew, and to belong to the same race as He should make anyone proud." He often expressed his love for the Jewish race as God's chosen people ...
>
> I must add that his denunciation of the Nazi persecution of Jews, the Nuremberg Laws against Jewry and all antisemitism, was worthy of his expressed love for Jewry, and another Jew and myself publicly thanked him for it.[134]

Another story from Siderman regarding his interaction with Jews in his audience is this:

> "I would like to see all my Jewish friends in the Church, for it is really their Church. It was a Jew who founded it, and the first Pope was a Jew. They really have a greater right to be in the Church than we Gentiles have!" and smiling down at two Jewish members of the audience whom he knew very well, he said, "Why don't you come into the Church? You know quite enough about it by now."

> One of the Jews smiled back at him and said, "Father McNabb thank you for the invitation, but I belong to the religion that Christ was born into and which he practiced, and if it was good enough for Christ to practice the Jewish religion as you say He did, then it can't be wrong for me to practice it, can it? So if you don't mind I'll stop where I am!" Naturally this started a further verbal battle that was carried on in good humor until the arrival of the next speaker.[135]

But, perhaps the most touching story, and one that certainly made an impression on Siderman, is the following that Siderman recounts:

> I would like to record an incident which I think typifies one of the great traits in his character, his humility. [At a meeting of the Catholic Guild of Israel, where he was invited to speak,] Each speaker in turn ended his address with the same words, "Forgive them Father for they know not what they do." Then it was Father Vincent's turn to speak. After some words on the Jews in relation to the founding of the Church, he said that "we were asking God to forgive the Jews for rejecting Christ, whilst we Catholics were daily committing the same sin of rejecting Christ. Christ had said that the Jews did not know what they were doing, but we Catholics *do* know," and, beating his breast, slowly and earnestly, he said, "Father forgive *ME*, for I know not what *I* do." There was a tense silence and then very slowly, he moved from the side of the platform where he had been standing, knelt before the Archbishop and kissed his ring.[136]

THE OPEN-AIR FORUMS at Marble Arch and Parliament Hill and other places throughout the city of London (Siderman came upon a crowd at a random street corner one day and was surprised and amused to see that Father Vincent was holding forth) were popular spots for education, debate and even entertainment. With no internet, no television, and with radio and cinema just burgeoning technologies, newspapers, journals, magazines, and books were the most common means for keeping up with current events and exploring intellectual matter. And with regard to specific issues, debates between leading men were common.

Given his abilities, Father Vincent had been engaging in debates from the time he was a young Friar. Perhaps the debate he was best known for was that with the prominent playwright, polemicist, communist and fellow Irishman, George Bernard Shaw, in 1931.

Shaw lived a varied and controversial life, and while he is best known as a playwright (widely considered among British dramatists as second only to Shakespeare), he was active in social and political causes over the decades of his long life, often espousing both popular and unpopular opinions, particularly, regarding the latter, his support for eugenics, his admiration for Stalin, and his railing against vaccines. He remained incredibly popular throughout his life, with his plays often taking up the topics of the day. His outspokenness on economic and social matters also appealed greatly to the socialist and communist spirit of the time. He won the Nobel

Prize for literature in 1925 and was at the height of his popularity when he was invited by Father Vincent to debate. The secretary of the Central Branch of the Distributist League had invited Father Vincent to give a talk to its membership on the topic Human Liberty. Father Vincent accepted, conditionally. He wanted G. B. Shaw in attendance. The secretary thus wrote the following invitation to Shaw:

> Father Vincent McNabb, O.P., S.T.M, has asked me to invite you to a lecture on Human Liberty which he will give at The Devereux, Devereux Court, WC 2. The lecture is on Friday, October 2nd [1931] and at 7:15 pm and is designed to remove the false notions which you have on the subject. There will be no fee and no publicity. All we can give you is truth.[137]

It is a remarkable invitation, baiting Shaw in the manner of a prizefight. Shaw was up to the challenge, writing back:

> A calligraphic ambiguity leaves me in doubt whether Fr. McNabb is to speak at one-fifteen or seven-fifteen on Friday. I shall assume seven unless you send me a correction to 4 Whitehall Court, SW1; but unless you make it eight-fifteen I am afraid it will be impossible for me to attend. But as my views have no taint of heresy Fr. McNabb will run the risk of being silenced if he ventures to question them.—G. B. Shaw[138]

Again, a remarkable response. I am not educated in the way of debates of that period, but I am struck by the bravado. These were men being men. That Father Vincent, a holy man, would begin the volley the way he did is surprising; it is possible, of course, that the secretary of the Distributist League employed the mechanism on his own to bait Shaw into an appearance, but nevertheless. Given my own obtuseness, particularly when thinking on my feet, the self-assuredness of Father Vincent to engage so publicly this way with someone so popular and who was so obviously capable, shows remarkable courage. Of course, he was no slouch himself and had been debating weekly at Marble Arch and other venues for many years by this point. Perhaps he had the comfort of knowing the Holy Spirit and St. Dominic were on his side.

As for the debate itself, the secretary recounts the atmosphere:

> On the Friday evening, though no public announcement had been made, I transferred the meeting from the little room at the Devereux to a larger one at Carr's across the Strand [and waited for Shaw outside the former, to escort him to the bigger venue.]
>
> The entry to the meeting was quite a moment. The room rose and applauded, for the fame of Shaw was then very great and all felt it generous of him to come to so small a meeting. He was introduced to Father Vincent—they had not, I think, previously met.

A bright discussion ensued. A summary of the evening was given by Mr. Patrick Cahill, who wrote:

> Father Vincent [supported the notion of] the freedom of the human will, a full conception of which, he said, came in with Christianity. Freewill was not the power of doing what one liked but of willing what one liked: of willing to will. From the freedom of the individual, he passed (less hurriedly than I do here) to the freedom of groups. Today we were threatened with a grave danger to liberty, of which there was a dearth even in ideal. There was some prospect, for instance, of an attempt by the State to use compulsory labour and introduce the barracks system of living. Between that and us there stood things: those things that a free man could grow or raise for the sustenance of his family from his own property. He concluded: "The natural safeguard of liberty is the family; and the natural safeguard of the family is the homestead."[139]

For Father Vincent, it all returned to family and to Nazareth. Given his leanings, of course, and his idealism, that a homestead would be pitched as the height of liberty and thus self-reliance, is no surprise. For all the pitched anticipation, it turned out that there was more agreement than disagreement, though not without a few moments. Mr. Cahill continues:

> On being invited to give his views, Mr. Shaw said that as he was entirely with what Fr. McNabb had said, he proposed

to wait until someone else disagreed in order that he might wipe the floor with the objector. The general discussion was brief, and there did not appear, to Mr. Shaw's express disappointment, any determinist of H. G. Wells's school.[140]

As seems not out of character, Shaw dismissed important differences between his camp and the opposing one. Shaw's views were, essentially, communistic, advocating for government control of work so that "liberty," the topic of discussion, and which for him seemed to mean "leisure" (the opportunities, but also the dangers of which we have already addressed in these pages) would be maximized. As a thinker and a playwright, this is perhaps understandable. Shaw also complemented the Catholic monastic tradition in its shared similarities to the Russian barracks system of living and working. Father Vincent thanked Shaw for his approach and for "having raised the debate to a higher level than he had anticipated."[141] But, he couldn't let the communist go unscathed. Cahill continues:

"He has spoken of my [Father Vincent's] monastic home. I remember once discussing matters with a Fabian [socialist] and telling him that, as I was a mendicant friar, I was a communist. That is why we friars have never wished for communism. We know what it is and know it must be a voluntary thing. I have enjoyed the company of happy men and had a roof over my head. What I claim is that the family, too, should have a cloister—a little cloister made sacred not only with love, but with plighted love."

Then each of the two protagonists, left that room where had been voiced the debate which is at the root of the world's division today: each to his home—the Communist to property, the friar to poverty in common.[142]

✠

A mere year later, Father Vincent took quite some offense at G. B. Shaw's just-published book, *The Adventures of the Black Girl in Her Search for God*, and was not at all quiet about it. The book was controversial on several fronts, particularly regarding religion. Shaw suggested, perhaps as symbolic and to get a rise, that, among other things, the Ten Commandments should be reversed, and that St. John the Evangelist was on drugs when he wrote the Apocalypse. Father Vincent was aghast at the attack and preached strongly against the book within a week, dismissing it as rubbish. In one address he wouldn't even mention the title. Father Vincent was not the only one to take the book on, and as often happens, the opposite of the desired outcome results; the outcry led to the book being reprinted multiple times because of the publicity.

Fr. Bernard Delany, a prominent Dominican and the first editor of *Blackfriars*, after Father Vincent's death, cited a strip of paper he found amongst Father Vincent's belongings addressing how he felt about Shaw and his book (ever frugal, he was known to use every bit of paper so as not to waste). The sentiment gives not only his thoughts about the book, but insight into his "process" for his public speaking. This piece is unusual in that most of his writing is for others, not as an account of an event. Was he proud of that moment, I wonder. Or was he writing it down as preparation for something more to be said about the subject later, perhaps. In any event, from his strips of paper:

> When speaking of Bernard Shaw's book, I protested against Shaw's description of the Apocalypse of St. John as the visions of a drug addict. Suppose I were to write to one of the daily newspapers as follows:
>
> *Dear Mr. Editor,*
>
> *The only scientific explanation of Mr. Shaw's book is that it was written by a drug addict. It was quite manifestly written under the influence of drugs.*
>
> If I sent that letter what would happen? Swift as lightning came an answer from someone in the crowd: "It would go into the wastepaper basket!" I answered: "And that's where the book ought have gone." But let us suppose the impossible and my letter gets printed, what would happen? "You'd be summonsed for libel." Yes: I mustn't libel Bernard Shaw, and quite right, too; but Bernard Shaw, it seems, is quite right to libel an accepted Apostle of God.[143]

But returning to Father Vincent's feet. The number of occasions on which his boots are referenced is many, and the variety of ways in which the boots are described is entertaining in itself. My great-aunt, Mary, whose father was Father Vincent's brother, Richard (who, along with my great-grandfather, were the two of the eleven to emigrate to America; Richard settled in Portland not far from where I currently live), described with humor her first impressions on meeting her uncle on a trip to London and his "awful heavy *brogues*." I had never heard the word before and looked it up. It is derived from the Irish word bróg, which means "shoe." Another of her comments I found surprising was that, and this would be late in his life, "he was practically toothless." He mentioned to Mary while they were "walking for miles" that his Superior thought, "it might be advisable to have some dental work done but he felt it was all foolishness as his Aunt Maria had lived to be ninety, and she hadn't any teeth, though she was able to chew the toughest of meat!"[144]

Mrs. Ada Elizabeth Chesterton had her own way of describing his boots, *seven-league*. Ada was the wife of Cecil Chesterton, Gilbert Keith's brother. Cecil was, like his brother, brilliant and an outspoken proponent of Distributism. He was said to be the ideological force behind the movement, and was a well-known journalist. He and Father Vincent spent considerable time together. His early death, in 1918, was unfortunate. Father

Vincent preached at Cecil's funeral, and Belloc referred to it as the greatest piece of sacred oratory he had ever heard. In attendance at the funeral was Maurice Baring, a prominent "man of letters" at the time. Twenty-five years hence, Baring published a poem in the 1943 August issue of *Blackfriars* inspired by the comments of an unbeliever friend and poet who had accompanied Baring to the funeral:

> A poet heard you preach and told me this:
> While listening to your argument unwind
> He seemed to leave the heavy world behind;
> And liberated in a bright abyss
> All burdens and all load and weight to shed;
> Uplifted like a leaf before the wind,
> Untrammelled in a region unconfined,
> He moved as lightly as the happy dead.
> And as you read the message of Our Lord
> You stumbled over the familiar word,
> As if the news now sudden to you came;
> As if you stood upon the holy ground
> Within the house filled with mighty sound
> And lit with Pentecostal tongues of flame.

Interestingly, this was not the only poem written about Father Vincent. The author of this next poem (perhaps more playful than professional) also shared a Chesterton connection. W. R. Titterton, previously mentioned as being on the receiving end of Father Vincent's ire, was G. K. Chesterton's first biographer.

> Gay—and a challenge—the voice was. Flame in the eyes.
> Friendly, loving the face was, artful and wise.
> Eager, alive was the figure, worn to the bone.
> But his smile was his own.
> Striding—Winged Victory—habited, swift through the streets
> Poised like a blithe benediction over retreats.
> Dubbing himself a poor sinner with the gift of the gab,
> Wedded to poverty, rich in his holiness, lowliness, lovingness.
> That was our master, our playmate, confessor, teacher and comforter,
> Vincent McNabb.[145]

Remarkable. But those boots. Father Vincent kept up with Ada, who was a force in her own right. She described his boots this way (though her recounting the figure he cut, and his reception among the children in the neighborhood, is much more poignant):

> When, from St. Dominic's Priory, he strode through Kentish Town, from every street and court and alley, children—like homing pigeons—clustered round him, tugging at his habit, reaching for his sleeve, joyous and unafraid. And so, garlanded and encircled, he traversed his parish. He was a vast walker and ... would cover half London in his *seven-league boots*, arriving at his destination dusty, mud-splashed, but quite radiant.[146]

A beautiful brief portrait of a beloved, joyous man. *Seven-league boots?* The term is from European folklore, in which the wearer is able to distance seven leagues [a league is how far one can walk in an hour] per step.

Yes, Father Vincent, indeed a giant.

✠

Hobnailed boots? It was how Fr. Valentine described them in a summary of Father Vincent's final days. In a touching and somehow uplifting account of Father Vincent's diagnosis of throat cancer, Fr. Valentine writes:

> Thereafter the news [of his death] leaked out. This pleased him. How better to gather the crowds for this final homily on the Happy Death? Reporters began to take great interest in St. Dominic's [Priory]. This was someone they all knew–a strange, medieval figure who tramped the streets of London, his feet heavy with *hobnailed boots* and his shoulders loaded with a knapsack. And now he was dying—but dying in such an odd way.[147]

It was an interesting time, and the words Fr. Valentine uses—*Happy Death*—are appropriate. Yes, indeed, he had prepared his whole life for this. [Happy was also how he was generally described after his death in a piece in Blackfriars titled, "God's Happy Warrior" by Fr. Delany, O.P.[148]] But dying in such an *odd* way? His instructions to his weekly *Summa* study group students upon letting them know his diagnosis was indicative of his approach. As Fr. Valentine writes:

> He asked them all to take out pencil and paper and to write down, at his dictation, the following prayer:
>
> O blessed Virgin Mary, Mother of Seven Sorrows and therefore cause of our Joy, beseech thy divine son that this miserable sinner and tomfool, Father Vincent McNabb, may die without having a long face and being a wet blanket.[149]

This was on the evening of 19th April 1943. He asked his students to say this prayer for him regularly. It seems they did, and it seems it worked. Father Vincent was determined to live his last weeks as he had lived his entire life, industriously. He continued his preaching, his teaching, his walking, which made those observing him, especially the local Press, all the more interested (and often to the bewilderment of Brother Porter at the Priory, who was constantly besieged with requests from the Press). Fr. Valentine continued:

> What could they [his fellow friars] do with a man like this? There he was staggering about the Priory determined to say Holy Mass and attend every community duty whilst he still had an ounce of energy in his emaciated body.[150]

In a letter to my great-grandfather, Patrick, Sr. Mary Vincent, Patrick and Vincent's sister (the youngest of the eleven), wrote descriptively of the almost exhilarating lead up to Father Vincent's death. It was simply more of the same—walking, preaching, hearing confessions, praying—but with this growing knowledge inside him, and around him among others, of what he had been preparing for his entire life now in sight.

While we're not quite ready to say goodbye to Fr. Vincent yet, it bears mentioning again, his final words, ever-present in his soul, and on his mind, and, indeed, on his lips throughout his life: "Lord, thou knowest I love Thee."[151]

✠

Lord, thou knowest I love thee. Are there any more beautiful words? Is there anything else the Lord wants from us? Should this not be ever-present on the lips of all of us? After all, what is the purpose of our existence? To know Him, to serve Him, to love Him. *Lord, thou knowest I love thee.*

The words were, again, true, but also a reminder. Father Vincent deeply desired heaven. His depth of faith would never allow him to not believe that the Lord knew this, but like a child, he sought his heavenly Father's approval. Like any good lover, he wanted the object of his love to know. Of course, his heavenly Father most certainly did.

✠

And finally, with regard to the various descriptions of his boots, the aforementioned Member of Parliament, Mr. Tom O'Brien, who so revered Father Vincent, following him about London to hear him speak, writes of Father Vincent's visit to the pub to speak about the problem of evil: "He was wearing a reasonably white habit, black-green hat and *clod-hopping* boots."[152]

The term *clodhopper*, meaning heavy and awkward, is more familiar than seven-league or brogues, but what was perhaps more interesting about the quote is the reference to his habit being *reasonably* white. This is another in a list of observations that others would make about the Friar whose mind was clearly on higher things.

Father Vincent was known for his habit, which consisted of a tunic, a cincture, a rosary, a scapular, a cappa, a white and or black capuce (hood) not always being clean. He slept in it. On the floor. Every night. Siderman tells the following story:

> The coarse hand-woven habit of black and white material which Fr. McNabb always wore and of which he was so proud, usually seemed somewhat grimy and in need of cleaning. More than once I heard a woman say that it could do with a wash and that she would be pleased to do it, if only she could get hold of it.
>
> But one Sunday in summer the famous habit looked different; somewhat cleaner but not yet quite clean. After reading a text from the Bible as he always did when commencing his lecture, he smiled down at us and said, "Do you notice anything different about me today?" and

> after a moment's pause, "I've washed my habit. It was getting rather dirty, but I don't think I've made a very good job of it, have I? 'Biddy' [an affectionate term for a working-class woman] would have made a much better job of it, but 'Biddy' knows how to do things while I can only talk. It's patchy, isn't it?—and you can't imagine the mess I made with all that water!" We were all smiling with him and the lady standing next to me remarked, "Poor Fr. McNabb, can you see him washing his habit! I'd have done it for him." I am sure many other women in his crowd would also have undertaken that task.[153]

His niece, Sr. Mary Magdalen, recounted family gatherings during the summer back in Portaferry, and how a friend of the family, a simple woman, named Katie, who loved Father Vincent very much, "always insisted on washing his habit when he came on a visit. She used to get quite wordy on the subject of 'the dirt of it.'"[154] And Fr. Valentine had the following to say:

> Father Vincent never troubled to change his habit whenever he got wet. Sometimes he would come straight into the choir [the sanctuary where the community prayed together] from a tramp in the pouring rain to recite Office with the rest of us. On one occasion he walked across London in a deluge from St. Dominic's in the north-west district to the Dominican Convent in Portobello Road, Notting Hill, to fulfill his duties as "ordinary confessor to the Sisters." On arriving he insisted on going straight into the Sanctuary to begin his conference [spiritual teaching.] As one of the sisters remarked afterwards, she couldn't attend to a word he was saying for watching the water dripping off his cappa and running down the steps.
>
> ... Again, he would never send his habit to the laundry. He felt very strongly about this.
>
> "The machine," he would say, "ruins clothes. Any housewife knows that garments need different treatment like children. She will wash the worn, darned and patched clothes very carefully, coaxing months and years out of them. But you can't expect a machine to be so discriminating. It washed the clothes quickly but ruins half of them."
>
> And he lived up to this belief, always washing his own clothes in the bath, a few paces from his room. He would

> pay special attention to his habit, splashing it about in the hot water and rubbing it liberally with carbolic soap. He made a great deal of noise, but the results were far from satisfactory. We used to tell him that his idea of washing was to rub out the mud patched and stains, and spread them evenly throughout the whole fabric. This was more or less true unless he had a gala day in preparation for some feast. But to see him in a clean, white habit was something of a community occasion. After his washing his habit, he would hang it near the cistern in the attic; but as often as not he would put it on again before it dried. On one occasion I saw him out it on when it was almost dripping wet.[155]

But perhaps my favorite story relating to Father Vincent and his habit relates to his manifest joy.

> He never closed his windows day or night, whatever the weather might be unless he had a visitor. He objected to clothes because they made him feel "too hot," and in his last years wore nothing whatsoever under his habit. During one arctic winter, for instance, when the snow was lying several inches deep in the quadrangle at St. Dominic's he suddenly took off his boots and stockings after Matins, tucked up his habit and went gamboling through the snow like a child paddling in the sea at Margate. Needless to say, we told him pretty plainly at recreation the following day that elderly gentlemen had no right to take such risks.[156]

As with most things relating to life itself, and Father Vincent in particular, there is depth. Father Vincent was, as we already know, notable in so many ways and his habit was certainly one of them—not just in its state of cleanliness, but in that he wore it always. He was proud of it, and that a part of London—Blackfriars—was named after his Order in that most visual aspect: the Dominican habit. It might come as a surprise that, amongst his brothers, always wearing the habit was unique to him. His fellow friars, unless they were engaged in a specific Dominic-related function outside the Priory, wore their clerical "blacks," indistinguishable from "secular" or "parish" priests, instead of the Dominican habit. Indeed, at that time it was against the law to wear even the priestly blacks in public, though that was rarely enforced. But Father Vincent chose to wear that Dominican habit he so loved for more than just representation of the Order. He wore it as spiritual protection. His niece, Sr. Margaret Mary, stated as much. She knew him better than most, and felt, "that his own shyness and reserve made him the public wearing of the habit at times quite agonizing."[157]

This is contrary to how some perceived his decision. Father Vincent, as previously mentioned, was frequently the object of derision. There were those who thought he was an attention seeker, or even a "play-actor." Fr. Valentine makes the valid point that most holy men and women try to blend in, not stand out. Father Vincent's habit surely made him stand out. But was it vanity or high self-regard? Fr. Valentine, who lived at the

Priory with Father Vincent for years, remarks:

> This argument has little cogency; and in fact could never have been put forward by any of Father Vincent's own brethren. Not one of them ever suspected or had any reason to say, or ever said, to my knowledge, that Father Vincent thought he was a holy man. They were too conscious of the nuisance he made of himself because he thought exactly the opposite.[158]

Again, this returns to Father Vincent's words to our Lord, ever-present, "Lord, thou knowest I love thee." It is increasingly clear that yes, he loved the Lord, gave his very life to Him. But that also, in a state of keen spiritual awareness, he knew his own frailty and unworthiness. And it is in this that one is, in fact, holy. But there was always torment in this; holy torment. Torment of desire. Torment of recognizing and having been touched by Love, True Love. Father Vincent knew God. And in every fiber of his being—and part of the fiber of his being was a literal fiber, the wool of his habit—he sought that.

And perhaps in God's adjudication of the matter, Fr. Bede, the prior at the time, after prayerful reflection, decided to insist Father Vincent wear the clerical blacks. Father Vincent, ever obedient, did not protest. As Father Vincent's blacks were moth eaten and in disrepair, Fr. Bede brought him to town to be outfitted. And Fr. Valentine summarizes the situation when the two of them went into the tailor shop this way:

> But even a clerical outfitter cannot measure a man who is clad merely in a Dominican habit. Another superior might have done one of several things. But Father Bede wasn't that kind of superior. He gave it up.[159]

✠

I recognize a spiritual anxiety in my own life. It would be similar, but different in essential ways, to that experienced by Father Vincent, who was more pure, steadfast and holy. Where our spiritual anxiety would intersect, I think, is in desire. The object of that desire, at least for me? From an early age, I have simply wanted . . . *peace*. That desire for peace is self-serving, in a way.

To be done with it, with responsibilities, but most of all, hurts; personal hurts, the hurts of others, the hurts of the world.

God is the object of that peace, and it is He who placed this desire in my soul, and it is gift. I have corrupted this desire through my own sins and failings. By youthful foolishness, by worldliness, by ego and pride. By a lack of understanding—or if not a full lack of understanding; I think I have always known that true peace exists solely in Him—by an inability to fully indulge the gift. There is spiritual progression, of course, that would account for some of that; it is as the psalmist pleads for God to please, "Forget the sins of my youth." There has always been recognition that that innermost longing can only be achieved through Him. *He* is peace.

This desire, this awareness, again, is gift from Him; from Him directly, and elevated through baptism and gifts of the Holy Spirit conferred upon confirmation; but it is also a gift from family. I am a Christian, a Catholic, because that is what I was born into and this is how I was raised. The faith was handed down to me not just through the McNabb family, but also through the Donovans, the McCarvills and the McDonalds, my other forebears. This spiritual legacy, too, is gift. Tremendous gift. It is why family, the domestic church, is so important, this basic unit of a rightly rooted society that is becoming so corrupted. We need to return to Nazareth, as Father Vincent would say. In Nazareth is found ... *peace.*

Authentic peace is anxiety's cure, and that peace is achieved through recognition of, and devotion to Him; and so I say, in my own regard, through my own desires and efforts, like Father Vincent, who was better and more worthy and did more for himself and for God and for the world, "Lord, thou knowest I love thee."

✠

One of my favorite stories about humility, a mother's ongoing love for her son and Irishness—mostly Irishness; that most blessed Irishness, in this case, so reserved—came after Father Vincent preached his first sermon as a priest.

Leading up to that, we are given great insight into the depth of relationship between him and his mother, through letters. His lifelong devotion to his mother is greatly taken up by Fr. Valentine in his biography. Being the youngest boy, frailer than his five older brothers, and having had the health scare (a benign tumor, originally misdiagnosed) at age fourteen that was thought to be terminal, this relationship was naturally inclined. It was a forthright relationship of great closeness, particularly spiritual. One letter, in particular, speaks to this. It relates to his mother's sufferings due to significant illness, and her response to that, and his. He was twenty years old and in the seminary at the time, and writes:

> On the whole, I think I was pleased to hear what you wrote, not because of the crosses which it evidences, but because of your evident resignation. You say you do not feel much disturbed because God does not act blindly and His greatest punishments are but proofs of His infinite love. I cannot tell you how glad I felt to know these were your feelings, dear mother. Too often mothers' love is but maternal, more natural than supernatural, more selfish than self-sacrificing. For you now it is almost a double duty to keep before your eye God's providence for has He not out of His great mercy given you a new lease of life and spared you to us all. Sufferings you may have and *will* if you love Him, yet they will be for your merit and reward.[160]

Such spiritual sympathy. And so rightly rooted. That a mother and son correspond this way is evidence of the depth of faith of the family—of the depth of *understanding*. The superfluousness of the present world has fallen away, and what was left was this great recognition of higher things.

It was around this time that Father Vincent was writing to his mother of his forthcoming ordination. The joy surrounding this event for both of them is evident. It is hard to put words to the exalted blessing of priestly vocation in any family, and particularly for a mother. Perhaps it is rooted in that greatest spiritual relationship and fostering, that between Mother Mary and Jesus. Father Vincent writes of his desire for her to be present at his ordination:

> You see, my dear mother, if I am like the rest of the novices and not extraordinarily wicked I ought to receive the priesthood in about two years. That indeed will be the crowning day of my life, but what could I think or how could I feel glad if you my dear mother were not there to double my joy by sharing it.[161]

And he echoes these sentiments in subsequent letters. And of his first Holy Mass, which would be said within a few days of ordination:

> I suppose it is natural for you to be near me and watching your son when he offers his first Mass. This first great sacrifice of the priest to God, no less than God to man, would seem an incomplete thing if the priest's mother, with the deepest claims on him were not present to offer her claims as a sacrifice, too. The whole priest must be offered up, not excepting those closest bonds linking mother and son, but how can the sacrifice be complete, she being way, who alone can bring forward the victim?[162]

And, regarding the general honor for a family,

> I need not ask you to pray but to keep on praying for me and to add prayers. Is not my priesthood a family affair? Something more than an honours? God's gifts, especially the call to the priesthood, have no parallel with what the world calls honours. Worldly favours sink into the grave, and there end. God's gifts are but beginning after eternity.[163]

In some ways, his almost pleading for her presence is surprising. Perhaps not so much when considering the muted send-off he received when leaving for the seminary six years prior. He wrote that he was surprised by the lack of emotion, only to learn years later that they all cried for hours after his leaving. They, and his mother in particular, did not want him to have any emotional misgivings upon his departure.

> I never knew until years after I had left my home that my going away was the sorrow of sorrows to those I left behind. I saw no shed tears, not even in my mother's eye. She made everything easy for me to go, as if it were the greatest joy of her life. Years after I heard that the house

> had hardly recovered from its tears for hours and hours. Even people like myself can be missed.[164]

✠

And it is in this light that Ann McNabb's reaction, below, to this first sermon should be viewed. His parents did, in fact, make the trip to Woodchester for the occasion. It was surely one of the great moments of their lives. I can imagine their pride and their joy, particularly Ann's, who had offered her son all those years ago to St. Joseph, with the words, "Do with him what you will." So meaningful was this offering to both of them that Father Vincent requested, in anticipation of her trip to the ordination, to obtain a picture of the statue of St. Joseph in St. Patrick's church in Portaferry where she had offered him. He requested that candles be lit in front of it.

And they were present at his first Holy Mass. After Mass, Father Vincent asked how his sermon was. Her reply, perhaps so surprising to modern ears, or to those privy to the depth of the spiritual correspondence between the two of them, was, when she looked at him and said, matter-of-factly, "It was no better than it should be."[165]

Oh, the laugh I had at that. Clearly, Father Vincent himself was amused—perhaps not in the moment—but years later when re-telling the story. It speaks to the steadfastness of that Irish mother, whose favored son was now a priest of God. Inside, her beaming could not have been brighter, but ever-mindful of even the priest's need for humility, she taught him yet another lesson.

✠

Father Vincent was greatly devoted to his other mother, Mary, and thus the Rosary. This would be natural, of course, first and foremost as he was a good and believing Catholic. Also, his devotion to his own mother would perhaps be a subconscious—or even conscious—motive for indulgence of our Sweet Mother. That he was a Dominican would be a reason, too. It is generally acknowledged within the Church that St.

Dominic had been given the Rosary by Mary, herself, in a vision. This was in response to his lack of success in preaching against the great heresy of the time, Albigensianism. The devotion paid immediate results and the twentieth century Dominican theologian, Fr. Reginald Garrigou-LaGrange, remarked, "What the word of the preacher was unable to do, the sweet prayer of the Hail Mary did for hearts."

The Rosary is powerful in many ways, and given his own humble beginnings, Father Vincent was keenly aware of the prominence amongst ordinary Catholics and the role it played in holiness. When talking about the differences between professed religious, and the laity, he said: "Most of the contemplatives I have met are in the world, and these have found union with God through the Rosary."[166] And Fr. Valentine himself remembers well Father Vincent's devotion and understanding. He writes:

> The Rosary, he used to tell us, is the safest and surest way to union with God through mental prayer. I once told him how a certain priest had tried to convince me that the Rosary was essentially a primer for beginners. He was almost speechless with indignation. The Rosary, he would say, is the perfect technique, and he often analysed it himself as such both in his sermons and writings. But what impressed him most was the prayerfulness of many of the faithful who had been taught or had grown up to pray to God through Mary. He would set them forth as an object lesson even to religious.[167]

Father Vincent over-and-over professed his reverence for the family. Surely, his experiences within his own large, devout family was formative, alongside the reinforcement of such resulting from his own great intellectual and spiritual gifts. He frequently cited prayer, and specifically the rosary as binding elements of family life. My family and I were made aware, just this past year, of Fr. Patrick Peyton, who popularized the motto, "The family that prays together, stays together." His is a remarkable story of faith and perseverance and will. And it moves me so deeply to know of his Irish roots. I am grateful for the Irish. I am grateful for the faith. I am grateful for that own legacy in my life. I am grateful for the export of that faith from Ireland. I am grateful for the vocations that that faith inspired in Ireland. I am grateful for the vocations that that faith inspired here amongst Irish Americans. I am grateful for that faith that is battered, both here and there, but still beats true.

In fighting the heresies of our time, and in deepening the prayer life of the faithful, and in providing spiritual protection for individuals and families, *Mother, Mary, pray for us! Venerable Patrick Peyton, pray for us! Father Vincent, pray for us!*

✠

But, of course, the Rosary is not the only prayer. Father Vincent, it should be no surprise, had a lot to say about prayer—and he composed many prayers for himself and for others. Fr. Valentine writes:

> it would be wrong to think that Father Vincent did not encourage all those who came under his influence to pray and to pray much. Most of his fulminations were directed against those who "pray from a love of prayer and not from the love of God."
>
> ... There was no pretentiousness about Father Vincent's own prayer. He loved the Sacred Liturgy. Every Sunday, year after year, he was to be seen assisting as deacon or subdeacon on the altar at St. Dominic's, London. His devotion to the choral recitation of the Office was a by-word amongst the brethren. Even as a dying man he would drag himself to choir to say Office with the community. At mental prayer he knelt bolt upright without any support saying the Rosary, caressing and ruminating on each bead.[168]

Prayer, in the Church, though, has been undertaught to the faithful. We do not pray as we should. I repeat, we do not pray as we should. The importance of prayer is often talked about, but not properly encouraged—by the hierarchy, from the pulpit, inside the home. One of Father Vincent's books was *The Craft of Prayer*, and I do believe the title says it all. I offer here just one prayer of his own crafting from that book, as it gives both insight into the mind and soul of the man, but also relatable opportunity for the rest of us:

> Our Father
>
> How often, O my Master, have I said, "Our Father who art in Heaven." It has been on my lips since childhood. When was it ever truly in my heart? I have often said, "Thy Will be done." How often have I at once said it and truly meant it? Have I not meant, "Thy Will be mine—bend things to my will?"
>
> Bend my stubborn will, my master. Make my lips truthful. May my prayer be a prayer of petition.
>
> May I desire what I say I desire; and may I desire as first what Thou hast put first—at the head of all desires. Thy Will; Thy Kingdom; and the hallowing of Thy Name.[169]

Father Vincent tells a story about the Little Sisters of the Poor in Newcastle-upon-Tyne, where the family moved to when he was in his early teens. The sisters cared for the indigent in the community; and many of those same indigent were frequently found at the McNabb family house when he was growing up. Through the sisters, his mother had made their acquaintance and a number were frequent and often unannounced guests. It was certainly the welcome of Ann McNabb that brought the needy in, but also, in my estimation, the welcome of a bustling family home that attracted them. He writes:

> Another form of charity was awakened in our home by the nearness of the Little Sisters of the Poor. The old men and women who were healthy enough and trustworthy enough to be allowed a day out soon found the hospitality of our kitchen—and our pantry. Our house became for them a sort of home from home. If they found they had an hour or so in hand before they need report to the gatekeeper of the Little Sisters, they invited themselves to "Mrs. McNabb's." They paid my mother and my father and the family the great compliment of taking them for granted. Perhaps they never knew what joy the family felt at seeing one or other (of either sex) sitting smoking by the kitchen fire, after having their tea... On my ordination to the priesthood these old men and women lifted up their hearts to God in prayer for the son of her who had so often, like a dear daughter, lessened for them the loneliness of a childless old age.[170]

It is a touching story, and I cannot help but think of my own family in this regard, and my wife in particular. One of the great compliments a family can be paid is that other people, especially young people, want to be around it. I say with humility that this is generally true for us, and is largely due to my blessed wife, who is adored by my children's friends, but the vitality of my home and its rootedness are not to be discounted.

This began years ago, when my children were in elementary and middle school and our visitors were mainly the children of African refugees and immigrants, amongst whom we lived in our diverse neighborhood. Some of these kids had been born here in Portland, and some were recent arrivals. All of them, no doubt, were appreciative of the full fridge and ample space of our home, living as they did in small apartments in subsidized housing. It is one of the great graces in our family life to be a part of the lives of so many of these now-grown kids and their families.

✠

In *Angela's Ashes*, Frank McCourt recounts quite a bit about the feet of the poor boys in Limerick, and how shoes were seen as a luxury. While there is no evidence of the barefootedness of the McNabb boys—and there were six of them, alongside five girls—one thing was clear, they lived a very modest life. Given the number of them, birthdays were not celebrated with gifts, as it would have been too expensive to recognize all thirteen members of the household.

But Irish feet. One of my favorite scenes from the movie is when the teacher rebukes the boys in the classroom for making fun of Frank's clumpy, oversize boots, which made me think, at the time, of Father Vincent's. Young Frank took off his boots in class and hid them due to the ridicule. The ridicule of what he was left with—his bare feet—grew even louder. The teacher caught on, and, God bless him, filled with that particular Irish temper, devotion and theatre, excoriated them, *"Our Lord has no shoes! He died shoeless! You don't see your Lord hanging on the cross wearing shoes, do ya?"*

And that, of course, quietened them down. If just till they got outside.

✠

In a family, we are to build each other up in many ways, but most of all, spiritually. There are many ways to do this. Faith begins with the parents, of course. They are the heads of the domestic church, and they are responsible for the health and well-being of their children; first and foremost, the health and well-being of their souls. That health and well-being is fostered through example, through love and through teaching. Regarding the last of these, it is important to again relate the words of the psalmist, "Drill this into your children." The language and imagery might cause trepidation for the modern parent, but I am guessing even modern parents realize, if not with regard to spiritual matters, then at least with regard to intellectual and practical matters, that children, left to their own determination, will flounder. Children should be taught the faith, both through learning and by example. That is a baseline, and there will be great flourishment from there.

One of the most touching moments in this regard was recounted by my great-grandfather, Patrick, to Father Vincent. Father Vincent writes:

> There was another book beloved of my mother which showed her instinctive appreciation of the best. Let me set it before my readers dramatically as a story, or sea-yarn, told me by my elder brother, Patrick, only last year. He said that when he went to sea first, as an apprentice, my mother got his "things ready." In the family my mother was looked upon as almost as much a seaman as my father. All preparations for the sea-outfit were left to her; even down to the packing of the sea-chest. This precious piece of sea furniture was rarely unpacked by the apprentice during the first few days after leaving port. When my brother found time to unpack it for the first time he found everything an apprentice needed for his ship-work. But carefully stowed amongst the other sea-kit he found [the book] "The Imitation of Christ." I can only guess what it meant to him then, because when, almost sixty years

> after, himself a father and a grandfather, he told it to me, it was told almost with tears.[171]

There is just so very much here, as well. That my great-grandfather so earnestly appreciated this classic spiritual work by the fifteenth century priest Thomas à Kempis is inspiring. That his faith was so important to him that this book and this act brought him to tears is so very touching. And that act itself, my great-great grandmother encouraging his spiritual well-being and nourishment—that is symbolic of the faith being handed down.

And in this regard, it was clear this extraordinary book was appreciated by the family. Incredibly, and poignantly, Father Vincent, during his novitiate, wrote a poem to his mother, *To My Dear Mother*, and sent it to her along with "a copy of the Imitation of Christ, which I had myself bound."[172]

And finally, I will say that I have had my own copy of the book for twenty years. In picking it up now, I see that it is the "Fr. Ronald Knox translation," which is regarded "by many teachers, writers and readers, to be the best English translation ever, and one that greatly enhances the life-changing insights of Thomas à Kempis."[173] This is the same Fr. Ronald Knox who knew Father Vincent quite well and said about him,

> Father Vincent is the only person I have ever known about whom I have felt, and said more than once, "He gives you some idea of what a saint must be like." There was a kind of light about his presence which didn't seem to be quite of this world.[174]

Strikingly full-circle.

✠

One reflection later in Father Vincent's life is particularly meaningful to me, and particularly beautiful, despite, or perhaps because of, the depth of its simplicity. He wrote:

> A few weeks ago, I welcomed a brother who had returned from the States. [This would have been my great-grandfather, Patrick, or Richard, the only two who had

> emigrated to the States.] Four of us gathered together—myself, my brother, a nun sister [Sr. Mary Vincent[175], née Annie] and a very old sister of mine [Georgina.] The youngest was aged 66 and the oldest 78.[176] There was quite an extraordinary sense of intimacy at that meeting; we called each other by the names of childhood. They would forget to call me Father Vincent and would call me by the boyhood name they used at home.[177]

I can envision the scene, the four of them gathering, all of them seniors. They wouldn't have known it at the time, of course, but within a few years all of them (except my great-grandfather, if he was the fourth) would pass on to their reward. What must it have been like, especially with the brother who was there from the States. These long lives, formed so deeply in another country, Ireland, in that tight family of eleven children, so distinct in their upbringing. One can surely guess the topics of their conversation darted from remembrances of years long past, of other family members, of their parents, and of current times, of bodily aches and pains, of current events. It would be safe to say, too, that much of that conversation would have been rooted in their faithful outlook, with two of them professed religious, and Father Vincent at the height of his fame. But still, they called him Joe. He was just Joe to them and while he was extraordinary, he was still just Joe, and given his own comments on that he appreciated that very much. It makes me consider my own situation, as one of five, and I hope that the relationships between my siblings and me grow stronger than they currently are; I have to say they are not as rooted in a common, practicable faith, and perhaps this explains a lot. And I am thinking, too, of my own children, and my desire for the four of them to be able to share such an intimate moment with each other as they near their own end.

CHESTERTON wrote an Introduction to Father Vincent's book, *Francis Thompson and Other Essays*. The introduction is quotable, of course, with that being Chesterton. Chesterton writes more about Father Vincent himself than any of the essays contained therein, and focuses on the nature of fame and popularity. His central point, and we would do well to remember this in our time of "social media influencers," those who are "famous for being famous," and the many among us whose public notoriety outweighs their contribution to the common good. While Chesterton writes, more for effect than anything, that, "next to no one has ever heard of Father Vincent McNabb today." His comparator was a politician,

> whose name could be seen scattered over numberless newspapers, in numberless headlines ... and [now, shortly after his death] whose name is already forgotten ... But I would say briefly and firmly that [Father Vincent McNabb] is one of the few great men I have met in my life [and] at least nobody who has ever met or saw or heard Fr. McNabb has ever forgotten him.[178]

It is high praise, of course. He makes the further statement—and this would serve to be the endorsement for the essays—that the world thus has a tendency to pay more attention to those who have taken a "vow of wealth ... those men who meant to die worth a million and did," while he prefers to pay more attention to the wisdom of the ones who have taken a vow of poverty instead.

I am guessing he used this device to not just endorse Father Vincent, with whom he was very close, but also the subject of the first essay of the collection, Francis Thompson. Chesterton said about Thompson after Thompson's death that "we lost the greatest poetic energy since Browning." Thompson was a poet, yes, but was also a medical school dropout, opium addict, and Catholic revert, who ultimately succumbed to tuberculosis after an unhealthy life, including several years on the streets of London. His poem, *The Hound of Heaven*, is rooted in his gratitude to God—in this case, the Hound—for never giving up on him. The poem is still popular today, embraced by those who have come back to the church, those who are seeking spiritual nourishment, and even by those who are merely attracted by the title. Over the decades, filmmakers, songwriters, playwrights and visual artists have adapted Thompson's words and message. Interestingly, in the monumental Supreme Court decision, Brown vs. The Board of Education, the phrase "with all deliberate speed" from the poem is used "for the remedy sought in desegregation."

In such an interesting and varied life, in such a public life, and a well-known life, despite what Chesterton may have said, Father Vincent met, in various ways and capacities, many well-known people of the day. But one, Francis Thompson, was unusual, in that they only *almost* met; at Thompson's deathbed, where Father Vincent was requested to go, but failed to. These are Father Vincent' words:

> In writing of Francis Thompson I feel I must have felt as Samuel Johnson when he stood through a day of pitiless rain in Uttoxeter's marketplace to make amends to a dead father. One afternoon Sister Mary Michael of St. John and St. Elizabeth's Hospital came to me in one of its wards and asked me to see a poor man who was dying. I asked her, as I was bound to ask, if he was at death's point—or if he had by name besought me. And then, God forgive me, I laid hold of the excuse, valid in law but discredited in the higher law of love, that I should be trespassing on another priest's fold and that I must hurry home to my own flock. That poor many dying almost unknown was one

> whom I would have walked barefoot a hundred miles to see—Francis Thompson. And I had refused to see him![179]

Father Vincent was hardly alone in his praise of Thompson, of course, but there was particular lived-appeal that attracted him; Thompson's living amongst the common man, and his absolute reverence for the mercy and power of God, and of his own unworthiness. It is this last aspect that perhaps spoke most deeply to Father Vincent. He writes, with great feeling:

> It was the boldness of Francis Thompson in an age of agnosticism and mammon to offer the incense of poetry to the true God. His poetry was as imperative as a *Credo*. You can hardly understand a line he wrote until you realize to your dismay that his sin is always before him, and he is at pains to lay it before his readers. Yet he knew and almost persuaded the self-elect to admit his Redeemer liveth. He would not own that his mind was narrowed by admitting the existence of the Infinite. He would not repent in sack-cloth and ashes that life had lost its colour because God of infinite personality and power pursued him with infinite love. He would not foolishly reject the splendid vision of God in man, Heaven on Earth, Infinity in a span, merely because some men with no light in their fancy nor song in their throat denied the thing they could not see, even though it was the desire of their heart and of the eternal hills.[180]

A beautiful, elegiac summary in its own right. What a death bed meeting might have been like between the two.

It may be said that Francis Thompson's poetry is ultimately about longing; both of Creator and created, one for the other, the essence of pure in the former, present only sporadically, oftentimes pathetically, even desperately, in the latter. Thompson's words were a release for the longings of his soul, of his regret for his waywardness, of his urge for his true desire. A lesser poet, himself, but bringing other gifts to bear, Father Vincent lived this emotion, too, this longing throughout much of his life. His desire for union was strong. His yearning for relief for himself and for others powered his days. He grew to become acutely aware of the state of his soul—the only thing that truly matters—and when he sinned, his regret was usually immediate and excruciating.

He wrote that he never missed a weekly confession from the time he was seven years old. He sinned. The sins of the holy are often dismissed as minor, or not worthy of confessing except only occasionally. Father Vincent himself said, with humor, that hearing the confession of the sisters was like "being nibbled to death by ducks," but he grew to know the ill-effects of the stain of even the smallest sin in the light of Him Who Is So Pure.

Father Vincent was a passionate man, and when he was early in his ministry, he could be prideful in debate. Fr. Valentine writes:

> I remember going to the Student Master, himself an Irishman, and asking: "Does Father Vincent love a fight or love fighting for the Truth?" He may have thought this a strange or even silly question, I don't know. But he paused for a moment and then said: "Well, I suppose both."[181]

I am reminded here of young Joe, the schoolboy, who would engage in debate with a classmate and when the classmate had submitted, he would offer to switch sides so he could win from the opposite angle, as well. Fr. Valentine continues:

> There can be no doubt, then, that Father Vincent in those days [earlier in his ministry] was far from being a humble man ... he himself made no secret of this in later years, when he lamented his overweening ambition as a young priest.[182]

A life spent authentically seeking Him, will bear fruit, of course. As time went on, Father Vincent became more aware of the state of his soul. It is what prompted him, at times, toward dramatic displays of repentance. In his eulogy, the Provincial of the English Province of the Dominicans, Fr. Hilary Carpenter, mentions Father Vincent's personal humility, "we whose feet he had kissed when he thought he had offended us, or worse still for us, when we had done him some hurt."[183]

One notable time was after he had made a scene amongst his brethren, refusing to concede his position. After what was surely a fitful night of sleep, the following day:

> We all went in procession to the church after dinner and as we waited after our prayers for a few moments to make a "visit," Father Vincent went into the middle of the choir and facing the tabernacle said:
>
> "Dear Fathers, I am sorry for being a scandal to the community and ask your forgiveness."
>
> Then he went down full length in *venia*, and stayed there till the Prior gave him the signal to rise.[184]

This anecdote from Siderman reveals similar compunction:

> Fr. McNabb was a great preacher, and was constantly in demand. One of the churches where he was often to be heard was the well-known Corpus Christi Church, Maiden Lane, London, popularly known as "The Actors' Church." He was preaching a course of sermons there, Sunday by Sunday, and on this particular Sunday something happened which must have been unique in that church and given those who witnesses it an insight into that strange personality standing there in the pulpit.
>
> He was preaching on some of the truths taught by the Catholic Church, and by contrast was pointing out rather strongly the errors of the Protestants, when suddenly he stopped and said, "O, my God!—I have been very uncharitable. Will you excuse me, brethren, while I ask for God's forgiveness." With that he knelt down in the pulpit, facing the altar, and in a loud pleading voice asked the Almighty's pardon for a sinner who had been uncharitable to those, who, although outside the Church, were nevertheless God's children and his brethren. Having said that, he got to his feet again, made his excuses and continued with his sermon.[185]

✠

Father Vincent, like many holy people, was not always easy to live with. And, like most who aspire spiritually and work at it, in his younger years he was prone to bouts of egoism and could be intransigent. The following is from Fr. Walter McCuskern, O.P.:

> I knew Father Vincent for more than forty years. In 1901, I received the habit from his hands and my first two years were spent under his rule as Prior at Woodchester.
>
> ... When I was a young novice he always inspired me with admiration, reverence and affection. I looked up to him as one who was already being recognized as a man of outstanding personality and brilliant mental gifts in a background of unusual holiness and rigorous asceticism. In many ways he stood out quite vividly in my mind as the ideal Dominican, a man on fire with the love of God and zeal for souls.
>
> And yet at times I was very puzzled. To my young mind there seemed to be certain traits in his character which were inconsistent with true holiness. He would say and do things that would seem to manifest an intense egoism and pride. He had a supreme confidence in himself and his special way of doing things, saying quite openly not only was his way the best way, it was the only way ... And yet, in contrast to this, in other ways he gave such an inspiring example of the religious life at its best; no one could have been more zealous in the interests of souls and he was always most regular and so obviously a man of prayer. In my memory, it was this side of him which seemed to outweigh the rest and to leave my admiration, reverence and affection for him unchanged.

Ultimately, McCuskern became Father Vincent's prior, and though occasionally the negatives would arise, but much less frequently. McCuskern's ultimate assessment is this:

> He gave so many convincing proofs of his real, underlying humility that there was no room for doubt as to his real sanctity; and my considered judgment after living with him for many years is that he was the nearest approach to a saint that it has ever been my privilege to live with.[186]

✠

Any good preacher must know the issues his flock is facing, and Father Vincent was keen to keep up with the times. He was diligent and studied government reports to get to the root of societal ills. It was in these reports that real information was gleaned, unadulterated, and also how the government was dealing with them. He used the information in his ministry, and in his preaching and debates. It was his view, of course, that the Church must take care of the souls of the people, but he was not anti-government and recognized the separation of responsibilities. He did want to know and understand, though, the issues at their source, because they impacted his ministry. Siderman recounts:

> He said he never read novels or fiction although he loved the classics and good poetry . . . "Do you know," he said, "I spend hours reading Government Blue Books, and White Papers, and Ministry of Health Reports and other official documents of the same kind. They are more exciting and interesting than any fiction because they deal with facts and figures about *real* people, and I am interested in real people like *you*," he said pointedly.[187]

And necessarily, he was also a consumer of the news of the day as it appeared in media and in the press—and was even a contributor, which we will get to in a moment. In his referring to the newspapers, though cheeky, there is a great deal of truth to his remark: "I read the Gospel, The Good News, on Sunday, and open the Daily Press on Monday to see what the Devil has been up to."[188]

He wrote frequently, according to Fr. Valentine, for "*The Morning Leader*—a London paper which has long ceased publication, and in the local press, particularly *The Stroud Journal*."[189] And as Siderman relates, he made broadcasts for the B.B.C.:

> He made several broadcasts during the war from the British Broadcasting Company's studio in London. Referring to these he said, "I do not like broadcasting. I would not do it, except that I am under authority and must obey my orders." He belittled his efforts as a broadcaster and said that he supposed most people would switch off their sets as soon as they heard him speak. "I would sooner come here and see and speak to you all. I have always loved people more than I have loved things."[190]

Though a consumer and a contributor, he also distrusted the

media and didn't simply sit on his hands. Given his knowledge and steadfastness and understanding of the world, and his vocation to bring people to Christ, he could not assent misinformation, particularly when souls are on the line. Siderman writes,

> He complained frequently that many times he had sent letters to the Press either in correction of some erroneous statement or to put forward his point of view one some matter of public importance, but that his letters were not published, and usually not even acknowledged. Even the Catholic papers, he said, often failed him this way. "I wonder why it is,' he reflected in mock surprise. 'Do you think that perhaps my views are too strong for them?"[191]

I am hardly a prodigious writer of Letters to the Editor, but I do write them in response to moral issues (most recently countering the aforementioned applause one opinion columnist put forth for the passage of legalize abortion in Ireland in the local paper. I will again mention the Irish government's own published statistic on the number of abortions performed that first year, 2019: 6,666). But there is one point that Father Vincent made that I have reflected on and honored ever since I read it more than twenty years ago, and that relates to anonymous letters. Siderman writes,

> He was indignant, too, at the publishing of anonymous letters in the Press, and said he never read articles or letters if people had not the courage to allow their name to be stated. "These letters are not worth reading. I always put my name to whatever I write so that people can know who it is from. Perhaps that is why they seldom publish my letters."[192]

One of the great problems of our times is how social media companies allow the anonymity of the contributors on social media, allowing people to hide under pseudonyms while offering all manner of vitriolic, often uneducated opinions. It is much the same as with messages that "disappear" after they are read on popular social media apps, that frustrates parents trying to keep track of their children. The angst and the anger. The devil is surely at work in this.

Our credit card statement ends on the third of each month, and nearly every month, late in the month, my wife and I try to hold off on purchases until after the third, as we pay our balance in full. A few days ago, my wife was looking at the sorry state of my current pair of sneakers (I wear sneakers, mostly, because of a bad back relating to a sports injury suffered decades ago), and suggested they need replacing. "I am not so sure they do," I said (in the aftermath of piling bills for tuition and Christmas and life), and I am wondering just how far I can make it without intervention. I am reminded of a story about Father Vincent being gifted boots by those who could not help but notice the need for their replacement. Siderman relates the following:

> His own poverty was often obvious. He had made a visit to the Men's Guild meeting on a bitterly cold wet night, and it was noticed by some that his boots had holes that were letting in the wet. In spite of his smiling protestations they insisted on taking his foot measurements, and duly presented him with a pair of boots, much to his embarrassment. His gratitude for this practical way of showing their esteem for him was almost overwhelming.[193]

And speaking of poverty and vows of poverty, another of my uncles was a priest. Fr. Thomas Donovan, S.J., was the brother of my grandmother, Ann. Ann was married to my grandfather, Joseph Vincent McNabb, Father Vincent's nephew. Uncle Tom was a character himself, part of that first generation of Irish American priests that for decades brought Irish devotion to this country. He taught at Boston College and Holy Cross, and was eccentric in his own right. A story has been told in my family about Uncle Tom passing by a dorm at Holy Cross when down came a bucket of water on his head, recompense from a group of students for a bad grade or some such thing.

One of the many things I remember about Uncle Tom was his talking about his vow of poverty, and how generous parishioners were wherever he went, often gifting him money at the holidays, which he would have to turn in to the Superior. As a child, I thought that greatly unfair, and half-thought he would tell this story each Christmas because he was deciding to give me the money instead of his Superior, but no.

In any event, I do know how generous people can be toward priests, and there is one particularly touching story Father Vincent tells of a poor old man trying to give him a gift. This man was not a Catholic, but the husband of a woman who had converted at least partly due to the influence of Father Vincent's preaching. She died after a tragic illness. Father Vincent presided at the funeral, and Siderman tells the following story:

> As he left the graveyard the husband approached him, gave him a flower from a funeral bouquet that Father McNabb had arranged from a pious benefactor, and asked him how he was planning to return to his Priory. The sky was thunderous, and rain was beginning to fall. Father McNabb replied that he planned to return as he had come – on foot. The husband – trebly poor now – pulled from his pocket enough money to pay for a cab: at first Father McNabb demurred and then he realised that this was the widower's mite. With tears in his eyes, he accepted the money. He never forgot this instance of simple charity. Of that, Father Vincent wrote:
>
> "Blessed are the poor! Few things have ever touched me more than that. Out of his poverty he offered me my fare. Imagine that coming from one who has not the faith. What am I to do when I see him next? To kiss his feet would be unworthy of him. I shall pray … that God may give him the consolation of the faith."[194]

ONE OF THE VERY MANY THINGS we fail to fully appreciate about our Creator is His sense of humor. I don't mean, necessarily, in the comedic sense—though, through the keenness of our intellect, which is from Him, and which, in some very small way must mimic His own, the powers of observation can render situations *funny*—this is more adequately expressed in our propensity for joy. In joy, there is laughter. In joy, there is lightheartedness. In joy, there is acknowledgement of goodness, of hopefulness. In joy, there is a particular type of love.

The joy of Father Vincent has been mentioned many times. It is, largely, the joy of *trust*, and is exemplified in his life in many different ways. For someone who was so involved in addressing the challenges and failings of the world, who was so close to suffering, who ministered to the poor, the ill, to those steeped in sin, and verbally battled so many who had unholy intentions, it would be easy to be cynical or depressed. But that would mean a rejection of the supernatural virtue of hope, and a succumbing to the evil one, who seeks to destroy all things, and to sow hopelessness and despair. In light of this, it is not so surprising, then, that Father Vincent should be so joyful, and in delightful and unexpected ways. Fr. Valentine writes:

> Many other stories are told about Father Vincent at Woodchester [in the early years of his ministry]—how he mounted a bicycle without a brake and rode down Priory Hill to find himself over the hedge on the other side of the main road in pretty good condition but

> with a shattered bicycle; how the children loved him and he would invite a boy to ride him pick-a-back and challenge Fr. Leo Moore similarly mounted, each boy trying to unseat the other; how he and Fr. Leo were known as David and Jonathan because they seemed to be inseparable; how he would take strawberries and cream over to the headmistress and her assistant to refresh them after a grueling day's teaching in the summer; how he fell through a hammock in old Mrs. Lewis's garden when he was similarly regaling himself; how the parishioners loved him and were scared of him at one and the same time; how they built him a parish-room off the school and called it St. Joseph's, and so on.[195]

And while he could be difficult to live with given his expectations for himself and for others, there was no one, according to Fr. Valentine, who could laugh at himself more easily:

> At Community recreation no one was teased more than Father Vincent. No holds were barred, as they say. He was teased about his habit: "Why didn't he go out like everyone else in Blacks?" He was teased about his sermons, even about his very asceticism. At all this he would laugh heartily and often return good humouredly to the fray by teasing others. By hook or by crook the community had to prevent him from mounting one of his "hobby horses" as we used to call them, during recreation, and for the most part we succeeded. I have seen visitors in the common room at St. Dominic's aghast at our seeming lack of reverence for one who for many was one of the great figures of our time. I am sure that no man ever took such a ragging from his own brethren, or took such pleasure in laughing with others at himself.[196] … [and given his wearing his home spun habit, and his being known through the streets of London,] His brethren called him, good-humoredly, the Mahatma Gandhi of Kentish town.[197]

Let us not forget the previously told anecdote of how after community prayer one time he took off his boots, "tucked up his habit and went gamboling through the snow like a child paddling in the sea at Margate."[198] Sometimes, his joy would land him in trouble. Fr. Valentine tells the following story:

> His personal habits of life were just as uncompromising. He neither smoked nor drank, but he did not expect others to follow his example. There was nothing of the puritan about him. Once, in the refectory at Hawkesyard, a lay brother inadvertently filled his glass with beer. To our surprise, Father Vincent picked it up, drained it, and then looked around the community with a smile, as much as to say, "Beer is still good even though I cannot drink it" And he couldn't. [Given lifelong gastrointestinal problems], That single indiscretions laid him low for several days with a bilious attack.
>
> ... [and with regard to those occasional attacks] Once, Fr. Bede Jarrett insisted that he should get right into bed [which for decades he refused to do], not just lie on top of it, and put on some pyjamas. As he hadn't any, Fr. Bede lent him his own. It was a sight for the gods to see the dear Mahatma sitting up in bed, all tidy and spruce, sipping a glass of brandy [to help stave off nausea], whilst the father who looked after him so faithfully and for whom he had a great affection, stood by and said: "Drink it up, Father Vincent. Don't pretend you don't like it. A little of what you fancy does you good!"[199]

Joy! This joy, this vivacity, is heartening, in ways big and small, and needs to be intentional in each of us, particularly in these times of great darkness and trouble. I, a father and husband, who get caught up in the anxieties of life, and whose great inclination is to control, not trust, need constant reminding.

There were many times that, given his insistence on walking, he nearly missed an appointment. But God always seemed to get him there on time. A fellow priest gave the following account to Siderman:

> Traveling one day to Downside Abbey by special train with Father McNabb, where he was to preach on Blessed Oliver Plunkett, all the other Pilgrims, on arrival at Midsomer Norton, joined motor coaches to complete the journey, but Father McNabb set off alone to cross the fields on foot. Five minutes before he was due to preach he had not arrived, and just as scouts were being sent out to discover

> him, in case he had met with a mishap, the venerable Dominican vaulted over a stile, to the amazement of many, and fulfilled his engagement with striking discourse.[200]

As interesting, to me, was what he might have said about that great Irish martyr.

✠

Father Vincent observed, "Nowadays, it seems that most people are anxious to see what they can get, not what they can give. Many will be judged by their response to the Commandment to 'Love thy Neighbour.'"[201]

My family is comfortable. We do not always think of ourselves this way, however. We live in a home that is valued above the median price of homes in the area. Our family income is greater than the median income for those in our area. Our prospects are good, though not without challenge. Things are stable. So why is it that we feel *less* comfortable than we should? I have long thought of the relativism of thought, and how we tend to compare ourselves not to those with less, but those with more.

I myself can succumb to this at times. And my children, too. They have many friends who are the children of refugees and immigrants, and they know, first-hand, the struggles and the deprivations these families face. We have helped. We help. But because they also have friends among those wealthier than us, those with second and third homes, who have nicer cars, go on expensive vacations, and for whom paying for college is hardly a concern, these are the ones they compare their situations to, and when considering what they will do in their adult lives, I frequently hear a response centering around money, and not love of neighbor or love of God (though I have pointed out that these things do not have to be mutually exclusive).

In an age of opportunity for great wealth and declining morals, the challenge to maintain a proper understanding is real. And it is more acute than when Father Vincent was alive. In his prescience, he saw the situation getting worse. Even then, he was aware of the challenges, and would frequently lament, "The evils are so great that only by the grace of God and the practice of 'heroic virtue' is it possible for people to lead a good life."[202]

So, remember, children. God first, and love, love, love.

IN THIS AGE OF CALLS for radical change regarding economic issues, particularly from the young, it is interesting to see how history repeats itself. Questions in this realm were often posed to Father Vincent on the platform of the Catholic Evidence Guild. Siderman writes:

> Questions arising from these matters were always readily forthcoming especially from those who did not see in religion any hope of changing economics of a social system against which they had revolted.

Father Vincent would do his best to address those with a purely secular understanding of the world, or with socialistic or communistic leanings, but,

> All [his explanations], did not persuade many of his questioners and objectors against their belief and insistence that only a drastic change in the social and economic system, brought about by the workers in the secular sphere and *not* the religious sphere of activity, could they achieve what they sought for themselves.[203]

Related to this, one of the great tragedies of our time is a lack of thinking. The Dominicans are an intellectual order, and those called to its number are inclined toward not just a depth of spirituality but a depth of thought. Given his belief in the divine origins of life, all thought, if honest and carried forward, would inevitably lead to Truth. The problem, of course, and particularly today in our age of zingers, 140-word thought pieces, and cancelling those you disagree with is that we do not *think*, or have lost our ability, or inclination, to do so properly.

In his eulogy ten years after Father Vincent's death, Fr. Hilary Carpenter reminisced, "Father Vincent encouraged thinking. Think of anything," he would say to us, "but for God's sake, *think*."[204]

Encouraging thinking is part of the process of formation for the Friars, who are schooled in the approach of St. Thomas Aquinas who, in his quest for understanding would consider, objectively, all sides of an argument. As Siderman noted, Father Vincent would instruct his students,

> You cannot learn by proxy. It is not easy to learn. First you must attend to what is being said and then try to understand –that is sometimes difficult—and lastly, reason it out, and come to a conclusion, that is, accept something as the result of reason.[205]

But it did not stop there, of course. As he was a preacher, everyone, in a way, was his student, and particularly those he engaged with from the stage of the Catholic Evidence Guild. He lamented a lack of thinking and remarked one time,

> There is a bankruptcy of thinking these days ... Some people are always uncertain when there is proof, and quite certain when there isn't proof. The highest act of the intellect is to know what to believe.[206]
>
> ... [But] he was not slow to appreciate a good and well thought out question ... "that was a good question ... you have been thinking ..."[207]

And in his own effort to encourage thought, he would occasionally put forth something outrageous or that was sure to raise the ire of his audience. Siderman writes,

> He would just smile and wait for the meeting to quieten down, and sometimes say, "I am glad I provoked you. It will make you think." But on leaving the platform he would never forget to say his "God bless you all, I humbly beg your pardon."[208]

✠

Father Vincent would frequently refer to London as *Babylondon,* a reference to the biblical city, Babylon, which was filled with wickedness and debauchery, and symbolized the evils and temptations of an urban society. He loved the people of London, of course, and couldn't help but partake of some aspects of the positive fruits of the place where he lived. Mrs. Cecil Chesterton remembered these words of his, "I pray that I may die in the streets. I have loved the London streets."[209]

And her own recollections of him in that city: "And that is where I shall always see him—striding along the pavement, his eyes ashine, his head held high: at once the people's champion and their lover."[210]

But he was always skeptical of city-life for the many reasons already set forth and was never shy about urging people to leave London for a different type of life. He was frequently confronted by the many objections to the practicality of this. One time, in his typically mirthful way, and with regard to his preferred mode of personal transport asked the audience rhetorically, "'How can I get out of London?' Begin with the simplest answer: 'Walk out.'"

✠

One of the lasting legacies of Father Vincent is the religious order of women, the Corpus Christi Carmelites. The Order was founded under the direction of Father Vincent in his Parish at Leicester in 1908. The Bishop of Nottingham at the time, Bishop Brindle, in encouraging a group of women to help him with the poor and suffering, gave approval for their organization on the Feast of Our Lady of Mount Carmel, July 16, 1908, with the following words: *"You will be poor, and you will be despised."*

The group started as Dominican tertiaries, studying and training under Father Vincent, and according to Fr. Valentine,

> These sisters owed their early training to Father Vincent. Under his guidance, they organized retreats for boys and

> girls, and helped in any way they could in the parish. Vocations amongst the girls who came under their influence were numerous.[211]

The Corpus Christi Sisters were so successful they were invited to the United States and later to Trinidad, West Indies, in 1919, where, a decade later, at the invitation of the Carmelite sisters, who were seeking a community to promote the charism of St. Therese of Lisieux, they formally became members of that Order. They are still in existence today and carry out their mission of promoting Christian unity through the Eucharist, spreading the Little Way of St. Therese, and praying fervently for priests. They have communities in England, the United States, St. Vincent, St. Lucia, Granada, Guyana, and Trinidad and Tobago.[212]

The sisters still, to this day, cite Father Vincent and his efforts as one of the reasons for their success,[213]and I cannot help but think of Jesus' words, "By [his] fruits you will know [him]."

✠

Another extraordinary event in Father Vincent's life was his removing a curse from a village near Woodchester, the home of the Dominican priory. Oddly, the curse was placed on the village by a Catholic priest, who suffered greatly at the hands of the local people, who were fervently anti-Catholic. A woman related the story to Fr. Valentine. He recounts their conversation:

> When Fr. Dominic Barbieri came, before the arrival of the Dominicans, he used to go about in his habit, and the children would follow him and the other Fathers, shouting insults:
>
> *Catholic, Catholic, Quack, Quack, Quack!*
> *Go to the devil and don't come back!*
>
> "What did Fr. Dominic say?" I asked.
>
> "I don't know his exact words, of course, but he turned around on one occasion when he was being insulted and prayed that God would allow no Catholic family to live in the village."

"Perhaps he didn't want Catholics to be pestered by their neighbours," I said.

"I don't know," said the lady, "but it is well known that no Catholic family ever did live in the village after that. Not till Father Vincent removed the curse."

"Did you see him do that?"

"Yes, as a matter of fact I did, quite by accident. It was during a Mission given by a Capuchin Father. I saw two altar boys going through the village, in cassocks and surplices. After them came Father Vincent in his habit and carrying a Holy Water bucket and a brush. He sprinkled the roadways and the houses. Father Vincent wasn't afraid of anything or anybody."

"And are there Catholics in Woodchester now?"

"Well, you know there are. Quite a number."[214]

Aligned with this is the account of the poet W. R. Titterton:

> Not long after that my first-born died, and Father Vincent was to meet us at the grave. It was raining hard as we stood there, and then out of the mist a bare-headed, habited figure came striding in thick army boots. Of course, that often happened. And it increased my understanding of him. He came home with us after the funeral and blessed our house. It had been haunted.[215]

✠

Of the many well-known and influential people Father Vincent met or influenced, one of particular note is Servant of God, Dorothy Day. Dorothy Day, an American, was an atheist, social activist and radical, who converted to the Catholic faith in the late 1920s. In 1932, she was given a copy of Father Vincent's essay, *Nazareth or Social Chaos,* by the Frenchman, Peter Maurin, and that essay would greatly influence the nature of her thought and her ongoing activism. She was immediately attracted to the concept of Distributism and would go on to be a strong proponent. She and Maurin founded the Catholic Worker Movement, and though controversial in some of her radicalism, her cause for canonization has recently been opened by the Catholic Church, and thus she is now referred to as Servant of God.

She would often cite Father Vincent's influence, mentioning him in her best-selling book of her conversion, *The Long Loneliness.* I was particularly gratified when I recently read an excerpt from notes of hers published in 1967 in the Catholic Worker that "on pilgrimage" to London, she was honored to give a talk at Father Vincent McNabb Hall.[216] I hadn't known such a place existed.

✠

We can assume Father Vincent received his reward from his heavenly King, but he also received an award from an earthly one, the King of Belgium. In 1891, as a newly ordained priest, Father Vincent was sent to the University of Louvain in Belgium to carry on his studies. After three years, he was awarded the degree of Lector in Sacred Theology. This advanced degree enabled him to teach his brethren in the classroom, which he did most ably. Those three years were formative in another way, inspiring in him a deep love for the country of Belgium itself. Two decades later, in the face of German aggression and ultimate invasion of that neutral country, Father Vincent wrote a series of essays centering around the situation in Belgium. These essays were compiled into a remarkable book, *Europe's Ewe Lamb, and Other Essays on the Great War.* He argued against the German invasion, sought relief for Belgium in practical ways, and, as is evident both in the title of the book, and in the words written therein, he had a deep devotion, even love, for this small nation.

The writing is eloquent and heartfelt and is remarkable in its variety and forcefulness. In the opening essay, *Europe's Ewe Lamb,* he begins,

> It is night, quiet in the shadows of these Midland Hills. Were it a night as those that have gone before, the quiet shadows would be a gentle summons to sleep. But tonight I cannot sleep. For today I have read and seen the horrors I have dreaded since a child. The DAY! I have heard the sobs of refugees from Belgium. I have seen eyes filled with tears, eyes but lately filled with horrors beyond weeping.[217]

He goes on in various essays to detail the situation, seek help, address leaders and provide context for and explication of Just War. In his essay, "Help Belgium," he writes:

> There never was a nation that needs help as Belgium now needs it. There never was a nation that helped itself throughout the ages as Belgium has helped herself. This staining of Belgium soil with redeeming blood is not the tragedy of the little ewe lamb of Europe.[218]

And in his essay, "Britain's Duty to Belgium," he lays out the case urging Britain to come to the defense of this pacifist country, so brutally attacked by Germany. He even writes an open letter to Kaiser Wilhelm, excoriating him. Father Vincent raised a tremendous amount of money for the Belgium Relief Fund, and for all of his efforts, in 1919, he received from the King of Belgium the honor of Chevalier of the Order of the Crown of Belgium.

Again, remarkable, for this humble priest, one of eleven, from the small seaside village of Portaferry, County Down.

✠

Moving on from his reward from that earthly king, another noteworthy encounter of Father Vincent's was with a pope—Pope Pius X (1903–14). This meeting, to me, is particularly gratifying, but I am left to wonder about the deeper feelings Father Vincent may have had. He writes simply of their brief encounter, and his reverence for this successor of Peter is obvious (and McNabbian, if you will). He writes the following:

> I was sent to Rome—the best way of going there! People go by all sorts of other ways. They miss being sent. I don't suppose I will ever be in Rome again. [He did try to go again, late in life, inspired by Belloc—on foot! His request was denied.] I shall never forget the month I spent in that home of my soul. All sorts of other interests were there but in my soul was a sense of being entirely at home. I went to see the Pope—Pius X. I knelt at his feet. He would not allow anyone to kiss his feet. It was a great deprivation for me. He touched the piece of hair on my forehead. That

> piece of hair is never going to come out! If you see me in my coffin, it will be standing up proudly still![219]

Pope Pius X and Father Vincent certainly shared similar views on Modernism. That—*On Modernism*—is, in fact, the title of his best-known encyclical, and the hallmark of his papacy. He rejected modernist interpretations of Catholic doctrine, promoting traditional devotional practices and orthodox theology. Like Father Vincent, he saw what was heading our way. Like Father Vincent, much of what he feared has sadly come to pass. Today, of course, he is held up by some, and decried by others. He was a great pope. A saint, in fact. Had, that day, one eventual saint touched the forehead of another?

I OFTEN walk for the sake of thinking or praying or clearing my head or for the simple enjoyment of it. I have wondered if Father Vincent ever took a walk simply for these purposes. I know that he did these things while he walked, of course. And because he was active and had many obligations and appointments, he was frequently walking and long-distances at that, but I wonder if he ever just said, as I do nearly daily, "going for a walk." I tend to doubt it.

I would break down the variety of my own intentional walks in the following way: woods, city, cemeteries. Over the years, given the variety of places I have lived in my adult life—Boston, New York, Newport, Rhode Island, Dublin, Ireland and Portland, Maine—there has been beautiful texture to all these different locations.

I was so pleased—so very, very pleased—to read that my great-great-grandmother, Ann, Father Vincent's mother, preferred walking in cemeteries to other types of walks, as I do, too. Father Vincent writes:

> Often my mother would take her daily walk in Elswick Cemetery rather than in the more inviting Elswick Park, which adjoined. As is usual in public cemeteries there was a part of Elswisck Cemetery, usually the least cared-for, where the paupers were buried. It was always my mother's favourite walk. There she would often be seen following the burial of some poor uncared for brother or sister of hers whom she had mothered and sistered with her prayers [this was in Newcastle, where many of the poor came to her home for help].[220]

It is beautiful and touching that she would participate, at least passively, in that corporal work of mercy, burying the dead. I am certain her prayers were powerful. But I am also certain her attraction to the cemetery extended beyond a chance burial. Who is not moved when walking in a cemetery to that ultimate reality that our lives are ephemeral? It is a great reminder. As Catholics, we are taught to never lose sight of our last end. The dates and the names and adornments on the headstones. There is a general cemetery here in Portland—Evergreen Cemetery—that is well kept and quite populous. It is the final resting place for many of the City's best-known inhabitants, statesmen and businessmen, and the regular folk as well. The cemetery is across the street from the Catholic school my children attended when they were young, and I have walked its grounds, as such, many, many times. I know it well. And I love it. I have taken a picture of the same tree, looking upward through its branches for more than a decade now, in all seasons. As peaceful, even beautiful, as that place is, there is nothing quite like a Catholic cemetery. Across the water in South Portland is Calvary Cemetery, and the feel is decidedly different. Irish and Italian names, mostly, with a smattering of other traditionally Catholic nationalities. The many, many crucifixes, crosses and statues of Mary and Jesus and the angels; idolatrous to some, perhaps, but so evocative of that other world, that next world, that next life. So touching is one particular area, where many children have been laid to rest. Certainly, this place has seen its tears, but there is this ever-present reminder of that which lies beyond this reality.

Another great-granduncle of mine, Richard McNabb—Father Vincent's brother, my great-grandfather Patrick's brother—is buried in this graveyard and I have visited his gravesite many times, wiping the lichen off the headstone occasionally and sometimes placing a small stone atop it. Two years ago, I visited my great-grandfather's grave just outside Boston with my family on a rainy Sunday, and it was just lovely. It had been many, many years since I had been there. He lived to the great old age of ninety. In terms of Richard's and Patrick's brother—the central character of this book—my one regret is that while living three months in London on a student exchange I failed to visit the gravesite of Father Vincent in the grounds of Kensal Green Cemetery. So young, so foolish.

✠

And speaking of Father Vincent's grave, as we wind this down, the essence of Father Vincent's ministry needs to be emphasized: love. Yes, love for God. Yes, love for souls. That love was exhibited in many ways, to God, Himself, and to people. But always, in his heart, it was the common people, the poor, whom he felt closest to. It wasn't just that their sufferings were so bare, or the imposition of unrighteous power held sway over their lives, but that they, themselves, were often close to God, and from them, he learned and gained strength, feeling their deprivation, knowing, at least in part, their struggles. He had grown up poor. He had taken a vow of poverty and embraced that in a way few of his brothers did. As Fr. Mark Heath, a fellow Dominican wrote:

> His room was bare. In it was a bed on which he never slept … and a chair on which he never sat … he had only one habit, the one he wore … he was poor, and as a result of it, he had a deep love, as the London Times reported it, for "all who could claim poverty."[221]

He said many times, "It is better to need little than to have much." Poverty was a choice; his choice, and he found great satisfaction and beauty in it, and it enabled him to relate to the challenges of so many he saw before him. He was often captivated and humbled by the decency of the poor, and the wisdom of so-called tramps, whose common sense, he said, was often greater than most university professors.

The following story of an old cockney woman who came to see Father Vincent at St. Dominic's seeking a little money exemplifies this beautifully. Fr. Valentine writes:

> One day Father Vincent came to my room.

"Father," he said, "did you wash your feet on Holy Thursday?"

What next, I thought. I said: "Yes, Father."

"So did I, dear Father. We both washed our feet before the Prior saw them at the *Mandatum* [the Holy Thursday ceremony where feet are symbolically washed]."

Then he began walking up and down the room, muttering: "I never felt so ashamed in all my life."

Eventually, I asked him what he was ashamed about.

"An old woman has just been to see me," he said. "A Catholic woman from Litchham Street. The poorest street in our parish. She wanted some money. But what did she give *me!*?"

"Well, Grannie," I said to her. "How are you?"

"Mustn't grumble," she said.

("You see, Father—mustn't grumble!")

"I suppose you have little to do these days, Grannie. What do you do with your time?"

"Oh, lots of things. And I got an 'obby.'

"A hobby?" I said.

"Yes, Father. Feet washing."

"Feet washing?"

"Well, you know, Father, when people get sick and poorly or old like some of the folks round us that 'asn't been up for a long time it's nice to 'ave someone come along and 'elp 'em."

"And what do you do?"

"I take a bucket of warm water and soap and things and I washes their feet. Just turn back the bedclothes. Nice and refreshing to 'ave your feet washed when you're poorly."Father Vincent stood and looked at me.

"Worth a couple of bob, wasn't it, dear Father," he said.[222]

She had said it so matter-of-factly, with no trace of pride. He was dumbfounded and ashamed. Here in front of him was that purest Christian charity, so unassuming.

Fr. Valentine remarks how Father Vincent loved this aspect of his parish. He had been offered one time by the Provincial to "go to a house of more formal [Liturgical] observance," which fit his own sensibilities better, but which would have taken him from that struggling population he so loved. He declined, saying, "I beg you to leave me here among the sinners."[223]

He was the best combination of Christian ideals. Orthodoxy and love. Love and orthodoxy. But most of all, love. This following quotation of his speaks so greatly to that best part of Pope Francis's approach today:

> We mustn't go out into the world as if the world were our enemy and we have to conquer it. It is like the poor wounded man on the way to Jericho; it is hungry, and we want to give it something to eat; thirsty and we want to give it something to drink; homeless, and we want to open the door and give it a lodging and a home.[224]

And there were other ways in which he shared the best aspect of Pope Francis's approach. Fr. Vincent landed himself in hot water several times—even with the Vatican—over his willingness to discuss the role of women in the Church, and his ardent desire for Christian unity.[225] He never stepped over the boundary of orthodoxy, but he was a thinker, and wanted to allow for *thinking.* Also, in his humility, he sometimes mimicked the current pope's ability to seek forgiveness for the Church, whether the need to do so is fully justified or not. Of course, there is more healing, more good accomplished if we are not so entrenched in defending our own actions to the very end. The following recollection of a convert to the faith—before his conversion, and which helped bring him into the Church—is a powerful example of this:

> One act struck me very forcibly. I had spoken on the injuries I supposed myself to have received from some Catholics, and at once he bowed his head before me three times in silence, his head touching the floor. As he was a tall man, this was a very striking action. I suppose it was a form of apology for any ill deeds (if really such) done to me by Catholics.[226]

At the same time, he was not afraid to speak up in disagreement in matters relating to the pope; the following particular instance would fly directly into the seeming willingness of Pope Francis today to simply forgive, with no requirement for change or even contrition. Siderman writes,

> Following the publication of the Pope's Five Peace Points [regarding a just solution to bring about peace during WWII], I asked Father McNabb if he would comment upon them. His reply was: "I cannot accept them as they stand; they are incomplete, as they do not include the Christian principle of punishment. People who do evil should be punished." More than once he expressed his fears that the Pope would be asked to act as Arbitrator. "I pray God that he will not be so foolish as to accept," he said.[227]

Ultimately, the essence of his approach and ministry was rooted in the salvation of souls, through the beautiful fruits of orthodoxy and love. Love and orthodoxy. Love.

✠

Though obviously moved by the woman who washed feet, Father Vincent was hardly removed from his own practice of the corporal works of mercy. Of the many instances of his visiting the sick, or giving time to lonely widows, the following is its own stark example of compassion, fortitude—but also of the fruits of his mother's influence. Fr. Valentine recounted the following:

> The last nine cases [a nurse friend] attended and nursed for Father Vincent were men and women suffering from cancer; the very last that of a man whose face had been eaten away by this disease. (The reader is spared the more gruesome details.) The hair on the left side of this man's face was long as he had not shaved for many months. After his death, Father Vincent asked for a razor. The daughters of the house had protested; but he told them not to worry. His old mother had taken him to visit the sick when he was a small boy, and he got over that fear long ago.[228]

In his ode to his mother, *Eleven, Thank God,* Father Vincent writes of this, of his mother taking him to visit, on one occasion, a woman suffering from breast cancer, and the shocking sight of it,

> how the old charwoman slowly undid some wrappings and bandages and showed the mother and her son the

> great yawning, festering wound that cancer had made in her breast . . . It was a mother's heart that even then may have been giving to her dedicated and beloved son his first lessons in how to be a priest of Him Who cured the outcast leper with his touch.[229]

And thus another example of Ann McNabb bearing fruit.

BUT LOVE. And love's great end. It must have been shortly into the New Year of 1943 that Father Vincent was given the diagnosis of throat cancer. That this would be the preacher's ailment should not be surprising; God frequently allows symbolic events, or takes away dear gifts or faculties, to help us on our journey home.

Father Vincent's journey invites a walking with, in love. His love for God and for man was evident. The fullness of that was realized through his Dominican vocation. The most profund summary of that appears below, as told by his niece, Sr. Mary Magdalen, O.P. (née Annie).

Sr. Mary Magdalen was, again, the daughter of his sister, Mary. Mary, the oldest of the eleven, had been like a mother to her siblings, and was so very influential in Father Vincent's life. She had introduced him to the Dominicans and had given him much encouragement in the spiritual life. Mary had died young, and had entrusted the spiritual care of her daughter, Annie, to Father Vincent, who assumed the responsibility with utter seriousness and devotion. His influence was obvious, of course: she became a Dominican nun. As she knelt before him the night before her final profession, seeking his blessing, he, perhaps overcome, revealed to her, "You will never know, dear child, what your soul has cost me."[230]

But, her story:

> As a young Temporary Professed Sister, I taught for some years at the Elementary School in Stroud. Usually our summer holidays did not coincide with the time of the

annual retreat. So, one year I was sent with another Sister to Brewood, where Father Vincent was giving the retreat. During the retreat I got permission to go to his room each day for a few minutes. On one occasion I told him how puzzled and even distressed I was about the queer idea people seemed to have of him in England. I told him that he was often referred to as a public man who was clever but singular, and even something of a fanatic. All this grieved me terribly, because it seemed such an entirely strange view of my uncle, whom I knew so well and loved. From the time I had entered religion, when very young, he had always seemed so easy to talk to. When with him I could get very close to God. His words were always very simple, and even sublime. He took me to God in a straightforward motherly way. Quite simple and natural. This I knew was the real Uncle Vincent.

So, one day when I went to see him during that retreat at Brewood I asked him: Why don't you let people see the other side of you? The real side. Why do you give so many the impression that you must get on a tub and shout and make an exhibition of yourself?

I do not remember whether to me in reply; but he suddenly jumped up and stood by the crucifix hanging in the room, looking at it and talking to Our Lord in almost passionate gasps. I may not have got his exact words, but as I remember, he said:

"Dominic looked at you and—you looked at him—why were you there?—your great love—he wanted to give you what you wanted—souls—souls—and I must follow Dominic—I must use every power I have got to win them for you."

With that he hurried out and upstairs; it was time for the morning conference, and I remember he gave us a wonderful conference on St. Dominic. Some of the older Sisters who were present said afterwards that they had never heard Father Vincent so moved.[231]

In this, so many things are evident. Father Vincent had his detractors. There were those who found his style unseemly, or self-promotional, or an act. He knew this. But this, his beloved niece, bringing her concern to him in this way, so obviously grieved, clearly stung. I am reminded of the hurt Padre Pio felt when he was taken from ministry, when people protested his presence at Pietrelcina. But Father Vincent's reaction is so—as was the man, himself—*unusual*; at least in a worldly context. And his subsequent action is evidence of his otherworldliness. He did not defend himself to his niece. He seemed to have not addressed her at all. He went straight to his Lord, straight to the crucified Jesus, the Jesus whom he loved, the Jesus whom he had given his life to. Their relationship is evident. The mystical intimacy. The love and trust.

His words at that crucifix bear repeating, encapsulating him, encapsulating his life.

> Dominic looked at you and—you looked at him—why were you there?—your great love—he wanted to give you what you wanted—souls—souls—and I must follow Dominic—I must use every power I have got to win them for you.[232]

Of course, Father Vincent responded to his fatal diagnosis with matter-of-fact ease. As Siderman recounts,

> His impending death did not deter him from his usual activities. As he himself said, "I shall not take death lying down." That indomitable spirit was not to be quenched by what was to overtake him, and so he carried on almost until the end …
>
> The person who seemed least concerned was Father Vincent himself, and he made light of it to all who spoke of him, especially the newspaper reporters who interviewed him. They wrote graphic stories in their papers under such headings as "Famous Catholic Priest who is getting ready to die"—"Well known Catholic Priest jokes of coming death", etc.[233]

But death, of course, was not a joke. No one knew this better than Father Vincent. What we see here is an *understanding* of death. An understanding of what death was not—the end. Let us remember his comforting words he spoke to his mother, all those years prior, at the age of twelve, when his sister Margaret was about to die. He assured his mother of Margaret's impending peace in heaven. Now, heaven was on *his* horizon. The reward for all those years of hard work and devotion.

The following few months were a wrap-up of sorts, as he began to tell people of his diagnosis, often stating how busy he was, and making light of his predicament. "Do you know," he said, "I've found dying is a fulltime job, and I have lots of preparations to make."[234]

Of what would be his last Good Friday, his prior and friend, Fr. Bernard Delany wrote:

> I remember, I was going to do the Stations [a huge affair in Hyde Park that Father Vincent led every year] for him, but I realised what joy it would give him to go for what would be the last time and I gave way to his wishes and he went—even walking part of the way. I remember how he rejected my suggestion of a taxi to take him. He said, "What!—Going to the *Stations* in a taxi, when our Lord walked with a Cross!"—That evening an old friend of Father Vincent phoned to his Priory to enquire if he had returned safely, and a voice filled with emotion replied, "Yes, but this will be his last Good Friday with us; he is *very* ill."[235]

One of the things he carried out to the very end was his beloved weekly *Summa* lecture. That class was not just dear to him, but to his students. Miss Dorothy Finlayson summarizes the situation:

> The students had asked for [him to teach Thomas's treatise to the angels] as the angels were so soon to be his companions, but he said to one of them "I don't know what sort angels they will put me among, dear child. I am not good enough to go among the good angels."
>
> At Father Vincent's last lecture on 7th June 1943, ten days before he died, there were present students who had attended his first *Summa* lecture in 1921. One student had missed only one lecture during the last eighteen years. His pupils came from every walk of life—civil servants, doctors, teachers, artists, milliners and cooks. Priests and nuns, non-Catholic clergymen were often among his audience. Indeed, among his many examination successes appeared the names of many who were not Catholics

> and of at least one atheist. To Father Vincent they were all "my students."[236]

In true form, when he was nearing his end, he posted on the door to the room where they met, "Father McNabb's class next week is cancelled because he will be dead." Which turned out to be true.[237]

✠

In his waning days, just a few weeks before his death, Father Vincent walked to Hyde Park and spoke from the platform of the Catholic Evidence Guild. A woman who was there wrote to Siderman and recounted the following:

> One Sunday afternoon, a very few weeks before Father McNabb, R.I.P., died, I was passing the Catholic Evidence Guild pitch in Hyde Park on my way to keep an appointment at Tyburn Convent, when I heard these words spoken by Father McNabb:
>
> *"Jesus Christ is Love . . . Love . . . Love."*
>
> The voice was low and weak, that of a very sick worn-out man. What struck me was that it was his own burning love for his Master that gave strength to those words. They burnt into me, and I can and will always hear them. It reminded me of what I had read about the Cure of Ars, that everyone in the huge crowds could hear his burning words although he was so weak that his voice was scarcely audible—and the crowd in Hyde Park that afternoon was a great one. I deem it a grace of God to have caught those words from Father McNabb. It is a meditation for a lifetime.[238]

It is clear to me that *Love* was residing so fully in him that the words he expressed on the platform that day were a *knowing,* an indwelling of Jesus's love at that very moment, a foretaste of what he had worked so hard to know—for himself, for others—during his remarkable life.

As WRITTEN at the beginning of this book, Father Vincent sought to preach even in death. His elaborate requests for his funeral perhaps make greater sense after this account of his life. Yes, they came by the hundreds, if not thousands to recognize him, this unusual, saintly man who had walked among them for so many years. Fr. Valentine thought the tribute which would have pleased him most came from an old grannie who stood in the crowd outside the Priory, awaiting his coffin. He wrote of the overheard conversation from the woman and her grandson:

> Boy: "'ere he comes Gran!"
> Grannie: "That's right, bless 'im! Take yer 'at orf, son."[239]

They would have witnessed his last testament, his dying words, which were not spoken, but written, on his coffin.

Lord, thou knowest I love Thee.

That much was clear. But it was God—as is the case with all of us—who loved him first. That first love—His love—is so far beyond our comprehension, so burning and righteous and knowing, that we are incapable, in this life, of knowing it fully; but that second love, the love that comes from family, is not. And that, at least partly, is what this book is about.

As Father Vincent's McNabb's great-grandnephew, I cannot help but return to the notion of family, of the particular Nazareth, if you will, he was reared in, of the nurturing he received there, of how formative it was in his life and in his vocation. And thus, I cannot help but return to his mother,

Ann McNabb, my great-great-grandmother, who was strong and brave and faithful, who had left New York at God's very urging to save her soul, and whose legacy lives on today.

Her offering of her son to St. Joseph at his baptism with the instructions, "Do with him what you will!" certainly paid dividends. Yes, St. Joseph did a lot with her son. I find it both symbolic and a little unsatisfactory that Father Vincent's last book, which he never completed, was of that great saint. Perhaps he was waiting to get to that place he so longed to walk in all his life, to obtain the very best details.

NOTES

1. Mark Heath, O.P., "Father Vincent McNabb: Priest, Preacher, Dominican," *Dominicana* 32 (June 1947), pp. 80–6, at p. 81.
2. *Ibid.*
3. *The Chesterton Review* 22/1 & 2, February and May 1996. Fr. Vincent McNabb "Special Issue", p. 233.
4. E. A. Siderman, *A Saint in Hyde Park*, Geoffrey Bles, 1950, p. 12.
5. *Ibid.*, p. 122.
6. Ferdinand Valentine, O.P., *Father Vincent McNabb, O.P., The Portrait of a Great Dominican*, Burnes & Oates, 1955, p. 264.
7. Heath, *Father Vincent McNabb*, p. 81.
8. "Father Vincent McNabb", Wikipedia.
9. Valentine, *Father Vincent McNabb*, p. 213.
10. Heath, *Father Vincent McNabb*, p. 86.
11. Fr. Vincent McNabb, O.P., *Eleven, Thank God*, Sheed & Ward, 1944, pp. 3–7.
12. Siderman, *A Saint in Hyde Park*, p. 106.
13. Very Rev. Fr. Hilary Carpenter, O.P., *Nazareth or Social Chaos*, Eulogy from June 17, 1953, IHS Press, 2009, xxiv.
14. Valentine, *Father Vincent McNabb*, p. 205.
15. Siderman, *A Saint in Hyde Park*, p. 152.
16. *Ibid.*, p. 85.
17. Valentine, *Father Vincent McNabb*, p. 172.
18. *Ibid.*, p. 202.
19. *Ibid.*, p. 84.
20. *Ibid.*, p. 36.
21. McNabb, *Eleven, Thank God*, p. 8.
22. *Ibid.*
23. *Ibid.*, pp. 29–30.
24. Valentine, *Father Vincent McNabb*, p. 115.
25. Siderman, *A Saint in Hyde Park*, p. 41.

26. Valentine, *Father Vincent McNabb*, p. 252.
27. *Ibid.*, p. 177.
28. Siderman, *A Saint in Hyde Park*, p. 30.
29. *Ibid.*, p. 31.
30. McNabb, *Eleven, Thank God*, pp. 13–14.
31. *Ibid.*, p. 14.
32. Valentine, *Father Vincent McNabb*, p. 250.
33. Siderman, *A Saint in Hyde Park*, p. 10.
34. Valentine, *Father Vincent McNabb*, p. 22.
35. *Ibid.*, p. 85.
36. Siderman, *A Saint in Hyde Park*, p. 26.
37. Valentine, *Father Vincent McNabb*, p. 15.
38. *Ibid.*, p. 9.
39. Siderman, *A Saint in Hyde Park*, p. 115.
40. Valentine, *Father Vincent McNabb*, p. 155.
41. McNabb, *Eleven, Thank God*, p. 34.
42. Bernard Delany, O.P., "Father Vincent McNabb, O.P.: 1868–1943," *Studies: An Irish Quarterly Review* 32/128 (Dec. 1943), pp. 487–94.
43. Siderman, *A Saint in Hyde Park*, p. 62.
44. McNabb, *Eleven, Thank God*, p. 32.
45. *Ibid.*, p. 33.
46. *Ibid.*
47. Valentine, *Father Vincent McNabb*, p. 21.
48. *Ibid.*, p. 154.
49. Siderman, *A Saint in Hyde Park*, p. 13.
50. Ministry of Health Statistics, 2019. Total of 6,666 abortions carried out under new legislation last year – *The Irish Times* (June 30, 2020).
51. Adapted from my unpublished memoir, "It's All True."
52. McNabb, *Eleven, Thank God*, p. 35.
53. Valentine, *Father Vincent McNabb*, p. 231.
54. *Ibid.*, p. 244.
55. McNabb, *Eleven, Thank God*, pp. 45–6.
56. Maria Cecilia Baij, O.S.B., *The Life of Saint Joseph as Manifested by Our Lord, Jesus Christ*, One Hundred One Foundation, 1997.
57. Michael Hennessy, "The Apostle of First Principles," The Hilaire

Belloc Blog. Nov. 2013. http://thehilairebellocblog.blogspot.com/2013/11/the-apostle-of-first-principles.html.

58. Siderman, *A Saint in Hyde Park*, p. 30.
59. Valentine, *Father Vincent McNabb*, p. 176.
60. *Blackfriars* 24/281 (August 1943), p. 289.
61. G. K. Chesterton, Introduction to Fr. Vincent McNabb, *Francis Thompson and Other Essays*, St. Dominic's Press, 1935.
62. Valentine, *Father Vincent McNabb*, p. 184. His meaning, Fr. Valentine goes on to explain, was: "Here was a priest who went through practically the livelong day in the presence of Christ."
63. Siderman, *A Saint in Hyde Park*, p. 33.
64. Dr. Tobias Lanz, Introduction, *Flee to the Fields: The Founding Papers of the Catholic Land Movement*, IHS Press, 2003, p. 7.
65. *Ibid.*, pp. 69–79.
66. Valentine, *Father Vincent McNabb*, p. 214.
67. From the author's short-story collection, *The Body of This*, Wiseblood Books, 2011; originally published by Rock & Sling, 2007.
68. Valentine, *Father Vincent McNabb*, pp. 278–9.
69. Thomas E. Woods, Jr., *The Church and the Market, a Catholic Defense of the Free Economy*, Lexington Books, 2005, p. 166.
70. Siderman, *A Saint in Hyde Park*, pp. 48–9.
71. *Ibid.*, p. 56.
72. Woods, *The Church and the Market*, p. 162.
73. St. Francis de Sales, *Introduction to the Devout Life*, ch. XXIII, "Of Forbidden Games."
74. Valentine, *Father Vincent McNabb*, pp. 24–5.
75. Lay Dominicans are allowed to be buried in the full habit of the Order. I have considered this for myself, but it doesn't seem right. My Dominican vocation is secondary to my calling to married life.
76. Valentine, *Father Vincent McNabb*, pp. 23–5.
77. *Ibid.*, p. 232.
78. *Ibid.*, pp. 232–3.
79. Siderman, *A Saint in Hyde Park*, pp. 122–3.
80. Valentine, *Father Vincent McNabb*, p. 184.
81. Siderman, *A Saint in Hyde Park*, p. 87.
82. *Ibid.*
83. Valentine, *Father Vincent McNabb*, p. 153.

84. *Ibid.*, p. 197.
85. *Ibid.*
86. Siderman, *A Saint in Hyde Park*, p. 151.
87. Heath, *Father Vincent McNabb*, p. 81.
88. *Harpers Magazine*, October 5, 2009, "Philosophers Rumble Over Van Gogh's Shoes."
89. Valentine, *Father Vincent McNabb*, p. xiv.
90. *Ibid.*
91. *Ibid.*
92. *Ibid.*, p. 133.
93. *Rerum Novarum*, May 15, 1891.
94. Valentine, *Father Vincent McNabb*, p. 122. Father Vincent was a voracious reader of government reports, as they gave indication of the state of affairs in society. This helped him to know what the masses were facing, and thus helped focus his ministry.
95. *Ibid.*
96. *Ibid.*, p. 123.
97. Valentine, *Father Vincent McNabb*, p. 294.
98. Siderman, *A Saint in Hyde Park*, p. 70.
99. Valentine, *Father Vincent McNabb*, pp. 195–6.
100. *Ibid.*, pp. 295–6.
101. *Ibid.*
102. *Ibid.*, p. 297.
103. *Ibid.*, p. 12.
104. *Ibid.*
105. Siderman, *A Saint in Hyde Park*, pp. 34–5.
106. *Ibid.*, p. 48.
107. *Ibid.*, p. 49.
108. Valentine, *Father Vincent McNabb*, pp. 36–7.
109. *Ibid.*, p. 286.
110. Siderman, *A Saint in Hyde Park*, p. 29.
111. *Ibid.*, p. 105.
112. Carpenter, *Nazareth or Social Chaos.*
113. *Ibid.*, pp. 18–19.
114. *Ibid.*
115. Valentine, *Father Vincent McNabb*, p. 154. While many outsiders

derided him as a "play-actor" in his approach, and considered his public acts of humility self-propping. One of the points Fr. Valentine makes is that his own brethren never doubted his low regard for himself (though some found his approach unseemly).

116. Siderman, *A Saint in Hyde Park*, p. 70.
117. McNabb, *Eleven, Thank God*, p. 2.
118. Valentine, *Father Vincent McNabb*, p. 235.
119. *Ibid.*, p. 234.
120. *Ibid.*, p. 235.
121. *Ibid.*, p. 15.
122. Andrew McNabb, *The Body of This.*
123. Valentine, *Father Vincent McNabb*, p. 235.
124. *Ibid.*, p. 230.
125. Siderman, *A Saint in Hyde Park*, p. 52.
126. *Ibid.*, pp. 87–8.
127. *Ibid.*, pp. 88–9.
128. *Ibid.*, p. 92–3.
129. *The Chesterton Review* 22/1 & 2, p. 206.
130. Siderman, *A Saint in Hyde Park*, p. 153.
131. *Ibid.*
132. *Ibid.*, book jacket/Introduction.
133. *Ibid.*, p. 104.
134. *Ibid.*, pp. 78–9.
135. *Ibid.*, p. 24.
136. *Ibid.*, p. 40.
137. Valentine, *Father Vincent McNabb*, p. 284.
138. *Ibid.*, p. 285.
139. *Ibid.*, pp. 284–5.
140. *Ibid.*
141. *Ibid.*, p. 285.
142. *Ibid.*
143. Siderman, *A Saint in Hyde Park*, pp. 157–8.
144. *Ibid.*, p. 256.
145. Valentine, *Father Vincent McNabb*, p. 280.
146. *Ibid.*
147. *Ibid.*, p. 203.

148. Fr Bernard Delaney, "God's Happy Warrior," *Blackfriars* 24/281 (1943), pp. 285–9.
149. *Ibid.*
150. *Ibid.*
151. Valentine, *Father Vincent McNabb*, p. 205.
152. *Ibid.*, p. 295.
153. Siderman, *A Saint in Hyde Park*, p. 59.
154. Valentine, *Father Vincent McNabb*, p. 242.
155. *Ibid.*, p. 164.
156. *Ibid.*, p. 163.
157. *Ibid.*, p. 246.
158. *Ibid.*, p. 166.
159. *Ibid.*, p. 167.
160. *Ibid.*, p. 47.
161. *Ibid.*, p. 49.
162. *Ibid.*, p. 55.
163. *Ibid.*, p. 56.
164. *Ibid.*, p. 40.
165. McNabb, *Eleven, Thank God*, p. 53.
166. Valentine, *Father Vincent McNabb*, p. 186.
167. *Ibid.*, pp. 187–8.
168. *Ibid.*, pp. 186–7.
169. Fr. Vincent McNabb, *The Craft of Prayer*, Burnes, Oates & Washburn, 1935, p. 47.
170. Valentine, *Father Vincent McNabb*, p. 180.
171. McNabb, *Eleven, Thank God*, pp. 31–2.
172. Valentine, *Father Vincent McNabb*, p. 57.
173. From the book jacket of Thomas à Kempis, *The Imitation of Christ*, Ignatius Press, 2005 (reprint of 1959, Burnes & Oates edition).
174. "Vincent McNabb," Wikipedia.
175. It is amazing that she took the second name, Vincent, presumably inspired by her brother. I have not come across mention of how Father Vincent took that name. Presumably Father Vincent Ferrer, O.P.
176. This would have been 1939, as Sr. Mary Vincent was present. She was the youngest in the family, and her birth year was 1873.
177. Valentine, *Father Vincent McNabb*, p. 231.

178. G. K. Chesterton, Introduction to Fr. Vincent McNabb, *Francis Thompson and Other Essays*, St. Dominic's Press, 1935.
179. *Ibid.*, p. 1.
180. *Ibid.*, p. 14.
181. Valentine, *Father Vincent McNabb*, p. 130.
182. *Ibid.*, p. 131.
183. Carpenter, *Nazareth or Social Chaos*, p. xxiii.
184. Valentine, *Father Vincent McNabb*, p. 305.
185. Siderman, *A Saint in Hyde Park*, pp. 35–6.
186. Valentine, *Father Vincent McNabb*, pp. 305–6.
187. Siderman, *A Saint in Hyde Park*, p. 15.
188. *Ibid.*, p. 104.
189. Valentine, *Father Vincent McNabb*, p. 105.
190. Siderman, *A Saint in Hyde Park*, p. 84.
191. *Ibid.*, pp. 99–100.
192. *Ibid.*, p. 32.
193. *Ibid.*, p. 118.
194. Valentine, *Father Vincent McNabb*, p. 230.
195. *Ibid.*, p. 111.
196. *Ibid.*, p. 168.
197. *Ibid.*, p. 157.
198. *Ibid.*, p. 163.
199. *Ibid.*, p. 157.
200. Siderman, *A Saint in Hyde Park*, p. 125.
201. *Ibid.*, p. 62.
202. *Ibid.*, p. 63.
203. *Ibid.*, pp. 62–3.
204. Carpenter, *Nazareth or Social Chaos*, p. xxv.
205. Siderman, *A Saint in Hyde Park*, p. 102.
206. *Ibid.*
207. *Ibid.*, p. 83.
208. *Ibid.*, pp. 103–4.
209. Valentine, *Father Vincent McNabb*, p. 283.
210. *Ibid.*, p. 283.
211. Valentine, *Father Vincent McNabb*, pp. 115–16.
212. Ocarmtt.org, the website of the Order, where they specifically

mention Father Vincent's influence.

213. Corpus Christi Carmelites—Our History—General Council (ocarmtt.org).
214. Valentine, *Father Vincent McNabb*, p. 110.
215. *Ibid.*, p. 279.
216. Dorothy Day, Catholic Worker Website, December 1967 Writing "On Pilgrimage."
217. Fr. Vincent McNabb, O.P., *Europe's Ewe Lamb and Other Essays on the Great War*, R. & T. Washbourne, 1916, p. 3.
218. *Ibid.*, p. 69.
219. Valentine, *Father Vincent McNabb*, p. 228.
220. *Ibid.*, pp. 180–1.
221. Heath, *Father Vincent McNabb*, p. 84.
222. Valentine, *Father Vincent McNabb*, p. 178.
223. *Ibid.*, p. 179.
224. *Ibid.*, p. 179 (quoting from The Very Reverend Fr. Vincent McNabb, *God's Way of Mercy*, Burnes, Oates & Washburn, 1937, p. 113).
225. Bede Bailey, O.P., "Fr. McNabb & Rome", *The Chesterton Review* 22/1 & 2 (1996), p. 125.
226. Siderman, *A Saint in Hyde Park*, p. 134.
227. *Ibid.*, p. 68.
228. Valentine, *Father Vincent McNabb*, pp. 108–9.
229. McNabb, *Eleven, Thank God*, p. 43.
230. Valentine, *Father Vincent McNabb*, p. 247.
231. *Ibid.*
232. *Ibid.*
233. Siderman, *A Saint in Hyde Park*, p. 149.
234. *Ibid.*, p. 150.
235. *Ibid.*, p. 147.
236. Valentine, *Father Vincent McNabb*, pp. 293–4.
237. Correspondence with Dermot Quinn, Editor, *The Chesterton Review*.
238. Siderman, *A Saint in Hyde Park*, p. 150.
239. Valentine, *Father Vincent McNabb*, p. 209.

www.ingramcontent.com/pod-product-compliance
Lightning Source LLC
Chambersburg PA
CBHW021058090426
42738CB00006B/398
* 9 7 8 0 8 5 2 4 4 7 1 1 6 *